CHRISTOPHER COLUMBUS
AND THE TAINO PEOPLE

THE HISTORY SMASHERS SERIES

The Mayflower

Women's Right to Vote

Pearl Harbor

The Titanic

The American Revolution

Plagues and Pandemics

The Underground Railroad

Christopher Columbus and the Taino People

HISTORY SMASHERS

CHRISTOPHER COLUMBUS AND THE TAINO PEOPLE

KATE MESSNER
AND JOSÉ BARREIRO

ILLUSTRATED BY FALYNN KOCH

RANDOM HOUSE 🏠 NEW YORK

Text copyright © 2023 by Kate Messner
Cover art copyright © 2023 by Dylan Meconis
Interior illustrations copyright © 2023 by Falynn Koch

All rights reserved. Published in the United States by
Random House Children's Books, a division of
Penguin Random House LLC, New York.

Random House and the colophon are registered trademarks of
Penguin Random House LLC.

Visit us on the Web! rhcbooks.com

Educators and librarians, for a variety of teaching tools, visit us at
RHTeachersLibrarians.com

Library of Congress Cataloging-in-Publication Data is available upon request.
ISBN 978-0-593-56426-4 (trade) | ISBN 978-0-593-56427-1 (lib. bdg.) |
ISBN 978-0-593-56428-8 (ebook)

Printed in the United States of America
10 9 8 7 6 5 4 3
First Edition

For our Taino ancestors, who struggled
to persevere, and for all my Taino people who
are still here, deeply planted and flowering.
Anjan katu!

—J.B.

For Patrice, who made history class a lot
more fun, and for everyone who asks
the tough questions

—K.M.

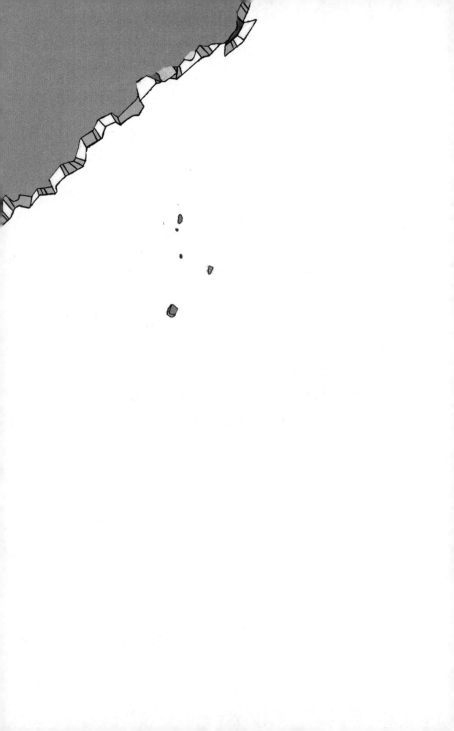

CONTENTS

You've probably heard the old rhyme "In 1492, Columbus sailed the ocean blue." Maybe you learned how Christopher Columbus set out to prove that the earth was round—not flat—or how he ended up "discovering" America. While it's true that Columbus crossed the Atlantic in 1492, many other tales about the famous explorer have been exaggerated or simply made up. Taino, and other Indigenous peoples who lived in the West Indies for thousands of years before Columbus arrived, are often left out of the story entirely.

The real story of Christopher Columbus is a lot more complicated than the myths. It's a story of nations seeking wealth and power, an explorer who didn't really understand the planet he was trying to explore, and the accidental discovery of a place unknown to Europeans. In the end, a voyage that almost didn't happen would change the world, enriching the lives of some people and destroying the lives of others. Here's the real deal about Columbus and the Taino people.

ONE
CHRISTOPHER COLUMBUS, MAN AND MYTH

The first thing most of us learn about Christopher Columbus is that he was an Italian explorer who discovered America. Those are the basics, right? The bare-bones facts about the world's most famous explorer. There's just one problem.

None of that is actually true.

For starters, Columbus never set foot in what is now the United States. His voyages took him to a number of islands in the Caribbean and along the coast of South America.

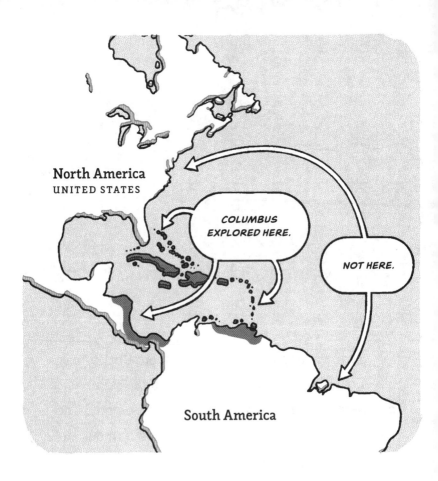

Columbus didn't "discover" those lands, either. Indigenous people, including the Taino people who met Columbus when he first arrived, had been living there for thousands of years, raising their families, running their societies, and trading with their neighbors. They owned their lands and homes. Saying that Columbus discovered their home is kind of like someone walking into your house and announcing that it's theirs now because they found it.

But even though Columbus didn't discover America, he was still a pretty big deal, right? Wasn't he the first person to sail across the Atlantic and visit the Western Hemisphere?

Actually, no.

Historians believe an explorer named Leif Erikson, who was born in Iceland, made the journey long before Columbus. Erikson is thought to have landed in what is now Newfoundland, Canada, around the year 1000 CE.

Leif Erikson Discovers America by Christian Krohg, 1893

Some historians have argued that African navigators likely voyaged across the Atlantic before Columbus, too. There are also legends about a monk named Brendan who set out from Ireland in a leather boat with some of his followers in the sixth century and might have reached what is now North America as well.

Given all that, just what is Christopher Columbus's claim to fame? He wasn't the first to cross the ocean or discover lands in the Western Hemisphere, but he did bring that part of the world to the attention of Europe for the first time. Many more explorers followed in his footsteps, beginning a new era of conquest and colonization.

So at least we can say that Columbus was an important Italian explorer, right?

Technically, no. Italy didn't exist as a country until 1861. But Columbus *was* born in the city of Genoa, which would eventually become part of Italy.

And what name do you think was written on the future explorer's birth certificate?

If you guessed Christopher Columbus, guess again.

His given name was Cristoforo Colombo. Different languages have different versions of popular names, and as Columbus traveled around Europe, he went by whatever form was common in each area. In Portugal, he was Cristóvão Colombo. In Spain, he called himself Cristóbal Colón. It was later that he became known in English as Christopher Columbus.

WHY SO MANY MYTHS?

Maybe you're wondering why people in the United States share so many stories about Christopher Columbus that aren't entirely true. It's because the explorer has become part of America's origin story.

You might know origin stories about how your favorite comic book and movie superheroes got their powers. Perhaps you've heard about the mystical herb of Wakanda that enhanced Black Panther's abilities, or the radioactive spider that bit Peter Parker, turning him into Spider-Man.

Origin stories aren't just for superheroes; entire countries can have them, too. These are widely shared stories about how a culture came to be and about how the people of a particular place came to have a shared identity. They can help a group feel unified, believing that they share a common history. Origin stories may be told in a way that exaggerates some details, makes up others, and leaves out big chunks of what really happened. Historians (and smart readers!) use documents, archaeology, and critical thinking to sort out the history from the myths.

We don't know a lot about the early years of Christopher Columbus because nobody realized he would turn out to be famous. The only documents about his early life came from events like his marriage and other family papers.

AS A YOUNG MAN, COLUMBUS DESCRIBED HIMSELF AS A WOOL WORKER. HE'D ALREADY BEGUN SAILING ON VOYAGES AND LEARNING THE SKILLS OF SEAFARING.

NO ONE'S SURE HOW COLUMBUS GOT TO PORTUGAL, BUT HIS SON HERNANDO WROTE THAT HE HAD QUITE AN ADVENTURE ON THE WAY.

1476

GENOA

LISBON

COLUMBUS WAS SUPPOSEDLY TRAVELING ON A MERCHANT SHIP WHEN A BATTLE BROKE OUT.

11

WHEN HIS SHIP CAUGHT FIRE, THE STORY GOES, COLUMBUS JUMPED INTO THE SEA, GRABBED AN OAR, AND STARTED SWIMMING.

THE BIOGRAPHY WRITTEN BY HIS SON SAYS COLUMBUS SWAM MORE THAN TWO LEAGUES.

THAT'S NEARLY **SEVEN MILES,** WHICH WOULD HAVE BEEN A HECK OF A SWIM.

COLUMBUS ENDED UP IN LISBON, PORTUGAL. THERE, FELLOW TRAVELERS FROM GENOA WELCOMED HIM, AND HE SETTLED IN, EVENTUALLY MARRYING A WOMAN NAMED FELIPA MONIZ.

IF YOU'RE A LITTLE SKEPTICAL ABOUT THAT LONG SWIM TO LISBON, YOU'RE NOT ALONE IN QUESTIONING THIS COLUMBUS BIOGRAPHY. THE SON WHO WROTE IT WASN'T BORN UNTIL AFTER THAT TRIP TO PORTUGAL. SO HOW DID HE GET THIS INFORMATION? DID COLUMBUS REALLY SWIM ALL THAT WAY? NO ONE KNOWS FOR SURE, BUT IT'S POSSIBLE THE STORY WAS EXAGGERATED TO MAKE THE EXPLORER LOOK MORE HEROIC.

Once Columbus got to Portugal, there are a few more paper trails we can follow to learn what happened to him there. We know he got married, and his son Diego was born in 1480. By then, Columbus could read and write Latin, which we know because some of his books contain notes written in that language. This gave Columbus more access to important books and educated society. There's also evidence to show that Columbus made a living on ships, sailing on voyages to Italy and dealing with different merchants.

WILL THE REAL CHRISTOPHER COLUMBUS PLEASE STAND UP?

No one knows exactly what Columbus looked like. We don't have any paintings of the explorer that were created while he was alive, so any portraits you've seen are just an artist's best guess. But we can assess how accurate those portraits are, based on descriptions of Columbus that were shared by people who knew him.

Portrait of a Man, Said to Be Christopher Columbus by Sebastiano del Piombo, 1519

Portrait of Gentleman, Said to Be Christopher Columbus by Lorenzo Lotto, 1512

One said he was handsome and well built, taller and stronger than average, with chestnut-brown hair and a ruddy (red-faced), blotchy complexion. Another called him "a man of tall and imposing stature, ruddy . . . of great intelligence, and with a long face." And one writer said Columbus had red hair "and the face somewhat flushed and freckled."

The biography attributed to Columbus's son also said the explorer was tall, with a long face, high cheekbones, an aquiline (hooked) nose, light-colored eyes, and fair hair that turned white when he aged. Based on the descriptions in these documents, how realistic do you think these paintings are?

Sometimes in illustrations, Columbus is drawn looking through a telescope. But that image needs a good smashing.

As you know by now, Columbus crossed the ocean in 1492. The telescope wasn't invented until 1608.

Columbus's father-in-law was a ship's captain who had explored the Atlantic islands west of Portugal, and he passed along some of his papers and maps to Columbus. The family had money and connections, and Columbus hoped that influence would help him gain support to explore an idea he'd been thinking about. He believed it was possible to reach the eastern lands of Asia and India by sailing west.

So this is the part of the story where we talk about how smart Columbus was, right? How he understood that the world was round, at a time when everybody else still thought it was flat?

Nope. Because that's another story that needs to be smashed.

By 1492, educated people knew the world was round. Ancient Greeks had figured that out centuries before Columbus was born. Philosopher and mathematician Pythagoras had suggested it way back in the sixth century BCE. By the fourth century BCE, the great philosopher Aristotle was pointing to real evidence to support the idea—the shadow of the earth on the moon and the curvature of the earth that sailors noticed when they approached land.

In the third century BCE, Eratosthenes used geometry to determine the earth's shape and approximate circumference. And in the second century CE, mathematician, astronomer, and geographer

Ptolemy wrote the *Almagest,* a book all about planet shapes and motions. By the time Columbus came along, that book was well known in Europe, and the idea of a round earth was common knowledge.

Columbus may have known that the earth was round, but he did a crummy job estimating its size. That's why so many people laughed at his idea to reach the east by sailing west. They understood that the earth was round, and they were also pretty sure that Columbus was wrong about how big it was.

In those days, there were lots of guesses flying around about the size of the earth. Some people thought it was bigger than it really is, while others imagined it was smaller. Most educated people thought the real answer was somewhere in the middle, close to Eratosthenes's estimate, which turned out to be pretty accurate.

But Columbus, who was really hoping the earth was smaller, chose to believe the low-end estimates. He guessed it was about 2,760 miles across the Atlantic from Portugal to Japan. In reality, it's about twelve thousand miles—a *much* longer trip! Based on that incorrect guess, Columbus was sure it would be a lot faster to go west than it would be to sail around the bottom of Africa, as other explorers were trying to do.

And just why were Europeans so intent on traveling to Asia? The answer to that question—and the story of what happened next—has to do with what the world looked like in 1491.

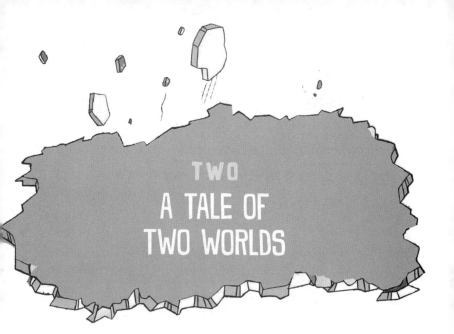

TWO
A TALE OF
TWO WORLDS

Sometimes when history books talk about European exploration, they refer to Europe as the "Old World" and the Americas as the "New World." But that's not really an accurate description, because it's based only on the perceptions of people who lived in Europe. Just because they didn't know about a continent doesn't mean that place and the people who lived there didn't exist. It wasn't suddenly "new" because they found out about it. People had been living there for thousands of years.

For a long time, historians thought the first people came to America by crossing a land bridge from

Asia at least 16,500 years ago. But in 2021, human footprints found in New Mexico's White Sands National Park were dated to be much older than that, showing that people have been in the Americas for at least twenty-one thousand to twenty-three thousand years.

Fossilized human footprints in White Sands National Park

The land bridge that once linked Asia and North America disappeared under the sea after the last ice age, around thirteen thousand years ago, leaving the people of Eurasia and North America isolated from one another.

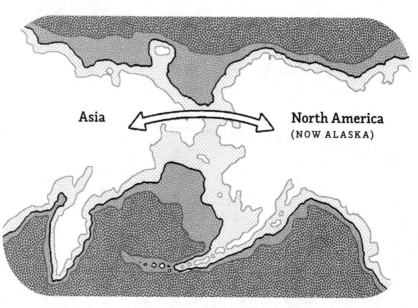

For thousands of years before Christopher Columbus arrived, the islands of the Caribbean Sea were the home of related peoples who are known to the world as Taino.

Taino communities were settled in thousands of villages on the islands of Cuba, Bohio (today called the Dominican Republic and Haiti), Boriken (today Puerto Rico), and Xaymaca (today Jamaica), and on the many small islands surrounding them, called keys. Taino were the most numerous Native people in the Caribbean, speaking the same language and sharing many traditions. The people who first met Columbus lived in the keys. They called themselves Lucayo, meaning "people of the keys," and spoke a version of the Taino language.

A LEGACY OF LANGUAGE

The Taino language is also sometimes called "Island Arawak." It emerged from the Arawak family of languages, which spread from the Amazonian world of South America into the Caribbean. The first Taino were Arawak people who traveled from Amazonian South America to the Caribbean thousands of years ago.

A number of modern-day English words are derived from the Taino. Taino people often traveled in boats called canoa, which became known in English as canoes. The word "key" comes to us from the Taino word "cay." The words "hurricane," "tobacco," and "hammock" also have their roots in the Taino language.

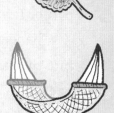

Columbus wrote that around every Taino house (called a bohio), there were flocks of tame ducks (yaguasa), which the kids raised for roasting on a wooden grill. This style of cooking was called barbacoa, which is the origin of the English word "barbecue."

The Taino people were, and are, Indigenous Americans. They built their lives and culture around their permanent home in the larger islands of the Caribbean. There, they enjoyed great forests, abundant freshwater rivers and streams, and coastal bays teeming with fish, game birds, and other sea life.

Over thousands of years, the Taino imagined and created a distinct way of life, a culture that grew into their sea and island world. Senior chiefs, or caciques, led nitainos, which were governing councils of family elders. Senior women and cacique women were part of Taino leadership.

The idea of strong, respected women was woven into the Taino belief system. Atabei and Itiba Cahubaba were Taino goddesses. They created spirits who made the ocean, governing the waters, winds, and nurturing powers of the Mother Earth.

Caciques and senior women organized the farming in Taino culture. Men were in charge of clearing and preparing fields, while women took charge of planting, harvesting, and food processing.

The Taino grew many foods, including yuca (manioc), which is a root crop more nutritious than potatoes. They also had a sweet potato called boniato, along with corn, beans, nuts, pineapple, and many other fruits. The Taino had excellent farming knowledge, including planting, harvesting, and food preservation techniques, some of which Native farmers in Cuba and the Dominican Republic still use today.

Taino people paid homage, in ceremony, to their main animal and plant food sources, as well as to natural forces like climate, season, and weather. They prayed and made food offerings to carvings of Yucahuguama, the grand spirit (cemi) of the yuca, of all agriculture, and of the sea.

Taino people believed in feeding everyone. The bounties of the earth were produced in cooperation and shared. The caciques were known to work alongside others in the yuca fields.

The Taino were also skilled sailors. They navigated the Caribbean in large boats, paddled by dozens of people. Each canoe was carefully designed and carved out from one very large tree trunk, with room enough for cargo, passengers, and eighty or more paddlers.

In this way, over thousands of years before Spain even existed, the Taino's ancestor people navigated their canoes north and west, between the many islands. It was nearly seven thousand years ago that the first canoes came from the Yucatán region, in what is now Mexico. And ever since, waves of people have navigated the sea. They came mostly from the northeast coast of South America (now Venezuela). These peoples are known by names such as Guana-hatabey, Ciboney, Ciguayo, and Carib (or Kalinago).

These various waves of Indigenous American

people brought seeds and agricultural knowledge, fishing and hunting techniques, distinct styles of pottery, useful tools, medicinal knowledge, and expertise in navigation. As they grew and developed their caciquedoms (chieftanships) as Taino people, their civilization and culture traveled from island to island. They also visited and traded with one another constantly, almost daily between Haiti and Cuba.

Taino men and some women also forded rivers and braved the ocean to hunt and fish. They hunted for abundant large tree rodents called jutia, as well as manatees, giant sea turtles called caguama, and

Taino along the coasts built large circular corrals made of reeds, which they kept filled with fish and turtles by the thousands.

many types of birds, including ducks, geese, and large parrots. They hunted for shellfish in the shallows and went out to sea for larger fish.

The Taino islands provided more than five thousand species of animals and plants, and the people made use of many of these. The jagua tree was used for dyeing cotton, while jocuma and guava trees were used to make rope. Taino people used the jucaro for underwater fish corrals and docks, and royal palms for building their large thatch-roofed homes. They used other trees and plants to make boats, spears, digging tools, chairs, bowls, baskets, woven mats, ropes, cloth for hammocks, and fishing nets.

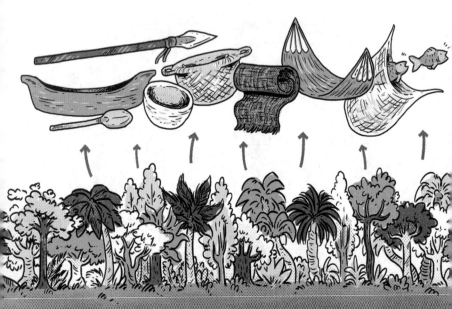

Taino people also developed hundreds of medicines from nature. They used massage and herbal remedies to treat digestive troubles, headaches, high blood pressure, fevers, and toothaches. Their use of medicines was part of their spirituality. Taino people would address the plants ceremonially, asking their permission and blessing for helping the sick.

The Taino world of 1491 was a thriving place. No one knows exactly how many Taino lived on all the islands, but there were likely one to two million people at the time they met Columbus. The Taino were among the most peaceful Native nations in the Americas, with only rare cases of conflict. It is true that Indigenous peoples of the Caribbean sometimes fought and took prisoners, but most often they visited and traded with one another in peace.

Meanwhile, on the other side of the ocean, Columbus would soon set sail under the flag of Spain, a nation that was no stranger to war and was aiming to expand its empire. The Silk Road, a long-established overland trade route from Europe to China, had closed in 1453. The spices that European people used to flavor and preserve their food were grown in India and on the islands of Southeast

Asia. They were much more difficult to get with that trade route shut down.

All over Europe, nations were searching for new routes to the East so merchants could bring back silk and spices and other goods. Portuguese explorers were trying to sail down the coast of Africa and around the Horn.

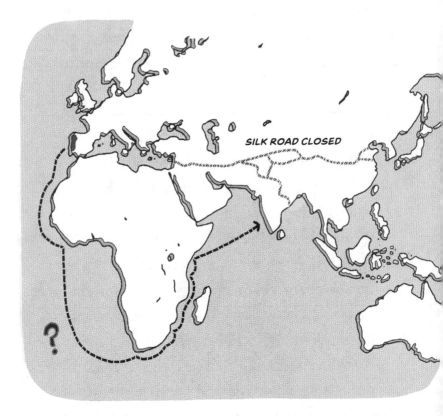

SILK ROAD CLOSED

But that was a long and dangerous journey. Columbus was sure he had the answer—sailing west, around the world, to reach India, China, and Japan.

Columbus owned a well-worn copy of a book called *The Travels of Marco Polo*. It's not about the swimming pool game; it's about a man named Marco Polo who traveled through China and India in the thirteenth century. He'd written about all the riches of Asia—silks and spices and palaces with roofs made of gold.

Those descriptions were enough to get anybody excited about exploration. European nations wanted those spices and other trade goods. They wanted gold. And they also wanted explorers to travel to new lands so they could convert the people who lived there to Christianity. (They didn't care if people who lived in those lands already had their own religions that they liked just fine.)

Columbus decided he was the guy who was going to find that new trade route, by setting out across the ocean. He had plenty of sailing experience. He knew how to captain a ship and navigate. And he knew how to deal with merchants, so he'd be all set once he arrived.

Columbus gets a lot of credit for being the first person to consider that it might be possible to reach the East by sailing west. But the truth is, he wasn't.

Italian geographer and mathematician Paolo dal Pozzo Toscanelli had the same thought, and he shared it with the king of Portugal in 1474. Other mariners had bounced the idea around, too, but never got support. And that turned out to be an issue for Columbus as well. He spent years running around Europe, asking different countries to pay for his trip. He started with the king of Portugal, who was funding voyages not only to find new trade routes, but also to claim more lands, take natural resources, and convert people to Christianity.

But when Columbus asked for support, the king said no. Maybe it was because he'd already given permission for another voyage to search for islands west of the Azores. The pilot of that ship had gone about 120 leagues—that's more than 400 miles—and didn't find anything. But the king of Portugal told Columbus to try asking him again later, maybe in a few years.

Columbus didn't want to wait. In 1485, he went to Spain, hoping that the Spanish king and queen, Ferdinand and Isabella, would be more interested in supporting his voyage. Columbus's wife had died, so he took his young son Diego with him to stay with family in Spain. Meanwhile, Columbus set to work trying to raise money for his trip.

36

HISTORIANS THINK IT WAS PROBABLY JANUARY 1486 BY THE TIME THEY AGREED TO SEE HIM.

THERE'S NO OFFICIAL REPORT OF WHAT HAPPENED AT THAT MEETING. ONE WRITER SAID COLUMBUS EXPLAINED HIS PLAN WITH A MAP OF THE WORLD.

GOLD!

THIS WAY!

KING FERDINAND AND QUEEN ISABELLA ORDERED A COMMISSION TO STUDY HIS REQUEST.

THE COMMISSION SENT WORD BACK TO THE KING AND QUEEN: THIS WAS NOT SOMETHING THEY SHOULD SUPPORT.

SORRY, COLUMBUS!

The king and queen, who were Catholic, were also busy fighting a series of battles against Muslims, called the Granada War, which lasted from 1482 to 1492. So they turned Columbus down, but they didn't give up on him entirely. In 1487, they started paying for his living expenses in Spain, even though they still weren't offering money for his voyage. During that time, Columbus met another woman and had a son named Hernando. (He's the son who would later write the questionable biography, including all those events from before he was born.) Columbus made a living by selling books and navigational charts while he kept nagging the royals for money.

Meanwhile, Portugal was making progress with

its explorations. In 1488, Bartolomeu Dias scored some major points when he became the first European to round the tip of Africa.

Columbus was sure he'd have the next big break-through, if only somebody would pay for his trip. But everywhere he went, people said no. Portugal had already turned him down. His brother Bartolomeo had tried to help out; he'd gone to England looking for

A sculpture of Portuguese explorer Bartolomeu Dias in London money for the trip, with no luck. And Spain just kept stringing him along.

After *seven years* of begging Ferdinand and Isabella for money, Columbus finally decided to call it a day and go to France. Maybe he'd find funding for his trip there.

But then the king and queen of Spain suddenly changed their minds. They sent a royal guard to find Columbus and summon him back to court. Again!

Why the change of heart? Many historians think the king and queen still didn't believe in Columbus's plan. But just in case he was right, they didn't want some other country getting all the benefits of his trip. Even if he couldn't find a new route to Asia, maybe he'd find something else worthwhile. The Spanish monarchs promised Columbus the rank of Admiral of the Ocean Sea, along with 10 percent of the revenues from any new lands he claimed for Spain.

Finally, the voyage was a go! They just had to find the money to pay for it.

JEWELS FOR SALE?

$ $ $ $ $

One of the often-told stories about Columbus's voyage is that Queen Isabella sold her jewels to pay for it. But that story needs a little smashing.

The biography of Columbus written by his son *does* say that the queen offered to sell her jewels to fund the voyage. But it turns out that she didn't have to. Her manager of accounts moved money around and came up with enough to send the explorer on his way. Columbus kicked in some funds for the trip, too—money that he likely borrowed from wealthy merchants who were hoping to get in on all those spices and riches if Columbus really did discover a new route to Asia.

Myths about Columbus talk about him as some kind of geography genius, but Columbus probably would have gotten a C in geography, at best. He was wrong about the size of the world and the location of Japan, among other things.

But he was incredibly persistent. He was good at making deals and drumming up support for himself, and that's how he ended up with the ships and money he needed to cross the ocean.

THREE
TO SEA!

You might think that once the Spanish king and queen decided to support Columbus, they'd go all out to make sure his trip was a success. But they only gave Columbus three ships, and none of them were very big.

There are no surviving plans for the ships, so we can't be sure what they looked like or how large they were. Columbus's diary didn't say much about them, other than that each ship had a little boat for going ashore and delivering messages between ships while they were at sea. Historians believe the largest of Columbus's ships was sixty to seventy feet long—about the length of a lane in a bowling alley—and had a crew of forty men. That's pretty close quarters!

NAME THAT SHIP

You can probably recite the names of Columbus's three ships—the *Niña,* the *Pinta,* and the *Santa Maria*. But those weren't the ships' original names.

Back in the 1400s, ships were often named after saints. The *Niña* was originally called the *Santa Clara* (Saint Clara) but was nicknamed the *Niña* after its owner, Juan Niño. Historians believe the *Pinta* may have also been named after a saint, but there's no record of its original name. *Pinta* was a nickname given by the sailors; it means "painted one." Columbus named the *Santa Maria*, but that ship had originally been called *La Gallega*, after the place where it was built.

Before he could set sail, Columbus needed a crew. There were plenty of mariners around Spain, earning a living by fishing. The trouble was, few of them were interested in such a long trip.

Columbus was all set to captain the *Santa Maria*. He convinced a shipowner named Martín Alonso Pinzón to command the *Pinta*. Martín's brother Vicente Yáñez Pinzón agreed to captain the *Niña*. The brothers were also in charge of finding a crew, but that was easier said than done.

According to a popular Columbus myth, sailors were afraid to join him because they all thought the world was flat. What if they sailed right off the edge? That story needs some serious smashing.

The sailors, like most people in Europe then, understood that you couldn't just fall off the edge of the earth. They did have other concerns about safety, though. Columbus was suggesting a route that hadn't been taken before, so there were real risks and dangers—everything from storms to diseases—with no promise of finding anything worthwhile.

Another myth that's sometimes told about Columbus is that the only sailors he could get were criminals. It's true that there were men on the first voyage who'd just been released from jail—but they were only three out of the ninety-man crew. One of them had been arrested for murdering a town crier, and the other two were accused of breaking the first guy out of jail. They were all offered shorter sentences if they'd go with Columbus, and they took the deal.

Within a month, Columbus and the Pinzón brothers had their crew signed up, and the ships were ready to go, loaded with a year's worth of supplies.

So what do we know about that famous first voyage? Most of it comes from a letter Columbus wrote to the king and queen of Spain, along with bits and pieces of his journal that were included in books written by others.

Columbus's original version is lost to history. But even if we had the whole journal, it's important to remember that primary sources like this aren't always entirely accurate. It's human nature for people to tell stories in ways that make them look good, downplaying their mistakes while emphasizing (and sometimes exaggerating) their successes. And people in history were no exception. Columbus would have written his journal entries knowing that they would likely become the official account of his trip—a voyage he hoped would make him wealthy and famous—so there was little incentive for him to record anything he did wrong.

Still, the excerpts and summaries of his journal that survived do give us a pretty good idea of what happened.

BEFORE SETTING OUT ACROSS THE ATLANTIC, ALL THREE SHIPS STOPPED IN THE CANARY ISLANDS, OFF THE COAST OF MOROCCO, TO PICK UP SUPPLIES.

SPAIN

MOROCCO

CANARY ISLANDS

AUGUST 3, 1492

ABOUT A MONTH LATER, IT WAS TIME TO SET SAIL.

SEPTEMBER 5, 1492

COLUMBUS MIGHT HAVE BEEN WRONG ABOUT THE SIZE OF THE EARTH, BUT HE DID HAVE A GOOD UNDERSTANDING OF THE WINDS AND CURRENTS OF THE EAST ATLANTIC.

SOME EARLIER PORTUGUESE VOYAGES THAT HAD LEFT FROM THE AZORES HAD TO TURN BACK BECAUSE OF WINDS. THE CANARY ISLANDS WERE A BETTER STARTING PLACE.

BUT THE VOYAGE WASN'T WITHOUT PROBLEMS. TWICE, THE PINTA'S RUDDER WAS DAMAGED.

COLUMBUS SUSPECTED SABOTAGE BY TWO SAILORS WHO HADN'T WANTED TO MAKE THE JOURNEY.

PSST PSST

HE TOLD HIS MEN TO SETTLE IN FOR A LONG TRIP; THEY WOULDN'T FIND LAND UNTIL THEY'D GONE 750 LEAGUES (ABOUT 2,600 MILES).

AFTER THEY'D GONE THAT FAR, THEY STOPPED SAILING AT NIGHT SO THEY WOULDN'T RISK RUNNING AGROUND.

COLUMBUS NAVIGATED BY DEAD RECKONING, AN APPROACH THAT USED DIRECTION, TIME, AND SPEED TO FIGURE OUT WHERE THEY WERE GOING.

SOME SAY COLUMBUS KEPT A FAKE SHIP'S LOG TO CONVINCE THE CREW THEY'D GONE LESS FAR THAN THEY REALLY HAD SO THEY WOULDN'T GET NERVOUS AND FREAK OUT.

COLUMBUS DID KEEP TWO LOGS, BUT HE PROBABLY WASN'T TRYING TO DUPE HIS CREW. HISTORIANS THINK IT'S MORE LIKELY THAT THE SECOND LOG USED A DIFFERENT METHOD FOR ESTIMATES ALONG THE WAY.

CONDITIONS ON THE SHIPS WERE CRAMPED. ONLY THE OFFICERS HAD AN ENCLOSED PLACE TO SLEEP AND KEEP THEIR THINGS.

THE REST OF THE CREW JUST HAD TO FIND A CORNER AND MAKE THE BEST OF IT.

MEALS USUALLY MEANT SHIP'S BISCUIT—BREAD BAKED TWICE TO DRY IT OUT SO IT WOULDN'T SPOIL—WITH DRIED, SALTED MEAT OR FISH.

THE ONLY WAY TO WASH UP WAS WITH A BUCKET OF SEAWATER . . .

. . . AND WHEN SAILORS HAD TO GO TO THE BATHROOM, THEY HUNG THEIR REAR ENDS OVER THE SIDE OF THE BOAT AND WIPED WITH A PIECE OF ROPE THAT DANGLED NEARBY.

By mid-September, the waters had grown calm, and sailors worried there might not even be enough wind to get back to Spain. Columbus just kept reassuring them it would all work out. He was certain they were close to the islands of Asia.

Sure enough, one night in late September, Martín Alonso Pinzón shouted from the *Pinta* that he'd seen land. Finally! It seemed to be less than a hundred miles to the southwest, so the ships changed course to head that way.

But in the morning, that land had disappeared! They thought it had just been a mirage, and there was nothing to do but keep sailing.

Columbus was worried. Had he already sailed past the islands they were looking for? Just how long would his crew hang in there? He was losing their support.

On October 6, the men on the *Santa Maria* decided they wanted out. They demanded to go back to Spain. Columbus summoned the ships to see what the other captains thought. Martín Alonso Pinzón told him not to give up and urged him to squash any thoughts of mutiny in the sailors who were starting to rebel.

Just what were the words that inspired Columbus to press on? Depends on who you ask. One witness to the conversation said it went like this:

YOUR LORDSHIP SHOULD HANG A HALF DOZEN OF THEM OR THROW THEM IN THE SEA, AND IF YOU DON'T DARE TO, MY BROTHER AND I WILL COME ALONGSIDE AND DO IT, FOR AN ARMADA THAT SAILED WITH THE MANDATE OF SUCH HIGH PRINCES CANNOT GO BACK WITHOUT GOOD NEWS.

Others suggested that Pinzón said something else:

ONWARD, ONWARD, FOR THIS IS AN ARMADA AND EMBASSY OF SUCH HIGH PRINCES AS OUR LORDS THE MONARCHS OF SPAIN.

Or maybe:

> GOD WILL GRANT US THE VICTORY TO DISCOVER LAND, FOR GOD WOULD NEVER WANT US TO RETURN IN SUCH SHAME.

Whatever he said, the message was clear: keep going. And that's what Columbus did.

THE NIÑA HAD SAILED AHEAD OF THE OTHER SHIPS, AND ON OCTOBER 7, THE CREW RAISED A FLAG AND FIRED A CANNON TO LET THE OTHERS KNOW THEY'D SEEN LAND.

BOOM

BUT WAS IT REAL THIS TIME? OR JUST ANOTHER MIRAGE?

THAT NIGHT, THE MEN SAW BIRDS FLYING TOWARD THE SOUTHWEST, SO COLUMBUS SET OFF IN THAT DIRECTION.

BUT DAYS PASSED, AND THERE WAS STILL NO LAND.

THE CREW GREW MORE AND MORE IMPATIENT. COLUMBUS WAS EVEN LOSING SUPPORT FROM HIS OTHER CAPTAINS. HOW WERE THEY EVER GOING TO GET BACK TO SPAIN WHEN THE WINDS KEPT BLOWING THEM WEST?

COLUMBUS SAID GOD HAD GIVEN THEM THE WEATHER THEY NEEDED TO GET THIS FAR, AND HE'D GIVE THEM THE WEATHER THEY NEEDED TO GET HOME.

THE CREW WASN'T SOLD ON THAT PLAN. THEY THREATENED MUTINY— AND FORCED COLUMBUS TO COMPROMISE.

HE PROMISED THEY'D GO ON JUST A FEW MORE DAYS, AND IF THEY DIDN'T FIND LAND, THEY'D TURN AROUND.

SOON THERE WERE MORE SIGNS OF LAND.

OCTOBER 11, 1492

THE NEXT NIGHT, A SAILOR ON THE PINTA SPOTTED A WHITE SAND BEACH IN THE MOONLIGHT.

LAND! LAND!

THEY HAD FINALLY MADE IT. BUT MADE IT TO WHERE?

Columbus and his crew waited for daylight to get closer to the islands. They didn't want to travel all that way only to slam into rocks in the dark. When the sun came up, they were ready to see Asia!

But the land before them wasn't what they were expecting. Where were the riches and spices? Where were the temples made of gold?

In reality, Columbus and his crew had landed in the islands now called the Bahamas. As the ships neared shore, people stood on the beach, watching them. What happened next would change those people's lives forever.

HEY, WHERE'S MY SILK JACKET?

Columbus had told his crew to keep their eyes open and promised ten thousand maravedis (the Spanish currency at the time) to the first person to see land. He even offered to throw in a nice silk jacket for extra incentive!

That sailor from the *Pinta* who first saw the beach was a man named Juan Rodríguez Bermejo, who was also known as Rodrigo de Triana. You're probably thinking he made out pretty well by being the first to spot land.

But Columbus then claimed that *he* was actually the first one who'd seen land. He said he'd spotted it the night before Bermejo and asked another man to confirm the sighting, but since that guy wasn't sure, they didn't alert the other ships.

So even though it was Bermejo who had alerted everyone, Columbus kept the reward for himself and didn't even give poor Bermejo the silk jacket.

FOUR
THE PEOPLE WHO DISCOVERED COLUMBUS

The people who greeted Columbus and his crew were, of course, the Taino. What did they think when Columbus and his men approached their shores? There's little doubt that the people on the beach would have marveled in curiosity at ships they'd never seen before. What were those big floating houses with flapping white sails like giant seagulls? European men would have looked strange to them, too, with clothes covering their whole bodies. Unlike the Taino men, they had facial hair and an abundance of body hair.

Young warrior-fishermen were sent to greet the

Spanish crew members who came ashore. The Taino men watched as Christopher Columbus himself planted a banner in the Taino sands. He spoke a language they did not understand, but in his words, Columbus claimed to take possession of all the new lands and places that he could see for the king and queen of Spain. The Spanish were especially interested in gold.

The *F* and the *Y* on the Spanish flag stand for the king and queen, Ferdinand and Isabella, or Ysabel in Spanish.

The Spanish described the Taino as uncivilized, but nothing could be further from the truth. One of the problems about our understanding of the Taino people is that much of our information came from the writings of Columbus, who wasn't Taino and didn't always understand what he was seeing and hearing. Pretty much any time Taino culture or customs were different from theirs, the European explorers decided that the Taino were "uncivilized" or "primitive." But from all early descriptions, even those written by the Spanish, the Taino were a healthy people who had sturdy houses and plenty to eat. They were organized and displayed gentle, hospitable customs.

At daybreak great multitudes of men came to the shore, all young and of fine shapes, very handsome . . . their eyes were large and very beautiful . . . They were straight-limbed without exception, and not with prominent bellies but handsomely shaped. . . .

They are free with all they possess . . . no one would believe it without having seen it. Of anything they have, if you ask them for it, they never say no; rather they invite you to share anything that they possess, and show as much love as if their hearts went with it. . . .

In other words: "These people are attractive. They're also really nice, and they're good at sharing!"

Even so, it wasn't long before Columbus was writing to the queen about where the Spanish might be able to build a fort for protection.

I saw a piece of land which is much like an island, though it is not one, on which there were six huts. It could be made into an island in two days, though I see no necessity to do so since these people are very unskilled in arms, as your Majesties will discover from seven whom I caused to be taken and brought aboard so that they may learn our language and return.

In other words: "I found some land we can make into a fort, but we probably won't even need it because these people aren't violent. You'll see that when you meet the seven people I kidnapped to bring back to Spain."

Columbus went on to tell the queen that the friendly, good-looking people he'd just met would be easy to enslave. Capturing people to enslave wasn't part of the original plan for Columbus's voyage. He was supposed to be trading spices and getting rich. But that hadn't worked out—at least not yet—so he was already looking for other ways to make the trip profitable.

However, should your Highnesses command it all the inhabitants could be taken away to Castile or held as slaves on the island, for which fifty men we could subjugate them all and make them do whatever we wish.

As soon as Columbus and his men met the Taino people, they judged them to be inferior, even less than human, since they weren't Christian, like the Spanish.

But the Taino people had their own beliefs. They understood their history through ancient tales that centered their own sacred beings and creation stories. The ancestors' history was oral, to be spoken and remembered, not written. Storytellers told and sang of how things came to be. In dances with long narrative songs, called areitos, Taino told their ancient stories of dangerous journeys at sea and of how the world was created.

TAINO CREATION STORIES ARE FOUNDATIONS OF CARIBBEAN INDIGENOUS IDENTITY. THEY REPRESENT THE SPIRITUAL MESSAGES AND BEINGS ABOUT WHOM THE TAINO PEOPLE SING IN SACRED CEREMONY.

THESE ANCIENT BEINGS ARE CALLED CEMIS, OR ZEMIS.

TAINO PEOPLE BELIEVE THESE ARE SACRED SPIRIT ANCESTORS WHO CREATED THE CARIBBEAN.

THE AREITOS NARRATE THE CREATION OF THE TAINO PEOPLE'S SEA, THEIR ISLAND LANDS, AND THEIR WORLD.

THEY TELL OF A MOTHER WHO DIED GIVING BIRTH TO QUADRUPLET SONS, KNOWN AS THE "FOUR TWINS," WHO WENT ON TO CREATE THE TAINO WORLD.

THE SONGS TELL OF HOW THE FOUR TWINS OBTAINED FIRE FOR THE TAINO . . .

. . . AND HOW THEY TOOK THEIR SACRED FOOD, THE HARDY CASABE (BREAD MADE FROM A ROOT VEGETABLE CALLED MANIOC, OR CASSAVA), FROM THE ORNERY GRANDFATHER, BAYAMANACO.

THE STORIES EXPLAIN HOW THE FOUR TWINS DANCED ON THE BACK OF A SACRED TURTLE TO EXPAND THE SOIL OF THE MOTHER EARTH FOR THE PEOPLE TO BUILD THEIR HOUSES.

THEY ALSO TELL OF A TIME WHEN THE SUN BURNED THE PEOPLE, WHO TOOK SHELTER IN CAVES.

WITH THE BURNING SUN BEHIND OVERCAST SKIES, THE PEOPLE LIVED IN THOSE CAVES FOR GENERATIONS.

FINALLY, AS THE SKY CLEARED AND THE SUN SHONE IN A WELCOMING WAY, THE TAINO PEOPLE EMERGED FROM THE MOTHER EARTH THROUGH TWO SACRED ORIGIN CAVES. ONE WAS FOR THE SUN AND THE MOON, AND ONE WAS FOR THE PEOPLE'S RE-EMERGENCE.

THESE CAVES WERE REMEMBERED IN CEREMONIAL SONGS, AND PEOPLE STILL KNOW WHERE THEY ARE.

Columbus and other European explorers believed a different creation story, the Bible's explanation of how God created the world in seven days. They demanded the right to convert the Taino people to their religion. At that time, spreading Christianity wasn't just a personal mission for Columbus; it was a major goal of European nations, replacing the Indigenous creation stories with their own.

In fact, the year after Columbus set sail, the pope, the leader of the Catholic Church, issued a special decree that became known as the Doctrine of Discovery.

It said European countries could claim, or take, any lands that were empty, and that included lands inhabited by people who weren't Christian. That meant the lands where the Taino had lived for thousands of years were considered "uninhabited" and fair game for explorers like Columbus. If you lived in one of those "uninhabited" places and someone from a European country showed up claiming to have discovered it, you were treated as a subject or a servant of that European nation and had to follow all of the new guy's rules. If you resisted, you could be declared a slave.

That was all part of the pope's decree. And Catholics of the time believed the pope never made mistakes, so if he said something, it had to be right. This doctrine guided European colonization, the process of taking control of a region and its resources, in the Americas and beyond.

Columbus wrote about differences between the Taino and the Spanish. He noted that the Taino people wore little or no clothing. This was shocking to the Spanish. The Taino had plenty of cotton, and they had the weaving and design ability to make clothes. Some of the caciques wore tunics or capes on ceremonial occasions, and on some islands, women wore short cotton skirts after marriage. Otherwise, the Taino wore no clothing, and that was natural because their climate was always warm, often very hot. For cooling and frequent bathing, Taino people spent much time in or around water. This cleansing custom was a type of ceremony.

You might think the Spanish would approve of that, since the Taino people were so clean. They'd see that as a good thing, right?

Nope. Instead, the Spanish passed a royal law *forbidding* the practice of bathing so often. They mistakenly believed that baths were somehow unhealthy.

Columbus and his men also noticed that the Taino had no iron weapons. Their tools were made of the natural resources surrounding them, such as conch shell, bone, clay, and different types of wood and stone. With these materials, they made tools to use for agriculture, hunting, navigation, and building homes. They also crafted beautiful works of ceremonial art, including sculpted statuettes that are still highly appreciated by Taino people and prized by collectors.

A Taino cemi of Deminán Caracaracol, 1200–1500 CE, Smithsonian National Museum of the American Indian

Many Europeans assumed the Taino were simple and weak because they avoided war and had no wish to conquer other peoples. Taino caciques would reportedly share their food and other resources to appease more warlike groups. A Taino leader, the cacique Guarionex, tried this peace-seeking tactic with Columbus and his men but found that they only wanted gold and were quick to take captives and enslave people.

Columbus and his crew explored several other nearby islands, looking for the riches of Asian king-doms (and not finding them) or sources of gold (and not finding that, either). But Columbus really wanted the Spanish monarchs to be excited about what he *had* found. He mentioned the small pieces of gold some Taino wore, but wrote in gushing terms about beautiful lagoons and lovely green trees bursting with fruits. His journals sometimes read like a travel ad for the islands.

The singing of small birds is so sweet that no one could ever wish to leave this place.

NAME THAT SERPENT

Sometimes, translations of Columbus's letters led to confusion. For a while, historians were wondering about a five-foot "sierpe," or serpent, that he reported seeing as he walked beside a lagoon.

October 21, 1492— I am bringing the skin to your Highnesses. As soon as we saw it, it swam into the lagoon and we followed it, for the water was not very deep, and we killed it with spears. It is almost five foot long and I believe there are many of them in this lagoon.

What species of snake could that have been? Or might it have been some kind of lizard? Historians actually believe neither is likely. In earlier diary passages, Columbus recorded seeing lizards, which he called "lagartos," as well as a snake, for which he used the word "culebra."

So what kind of animal *was* this serpent?

Modern experts now believe Columbus was probably writing about a crocodile.

The answer came from a crocodile bone discovered on Crooked Island, in the ruins of a village Columbus was believed to have visited. It was the first such evidence of crocodiles in the Bahamas. Until then, historians had been wondering if Columbus's serpent was a giant iguana, which could grow to that size but would have been less likely to swim into the lagoon.

When some Taino people told Columbus about a large island full of riches, he felt sure they were talking about Cipango. (That's what Marco Polo called Japan.) So Columbus set out to find it.

(Spoiler: It wasn't Japan.)

He actually landed on the island of Cuba on October 28 and noticed Taino people wearing small gold nose rings. Columbus indicated his interest in the gold pieces, offering many new things to the Taino and asking for more gold.

At that point, Columbus decided that Cuba must be part of mainland Asia. (The local people had already told him it was an island, but he argued that they were wrong and always maintained that he was right.) The Spanish men showed the islanders samples of what they were looking for—spices such as cinnamon and pepper, along with gold and pearls. They asked (in a language the islanders didn't understand) where they could find those things. They thought the islanders were telling them that the resources they wanted were off to the southeast. And they'd find a trading center with large ships there, too!

That all sounded great to Columbus, so off he went. From Cuba, Columbus headed for the island of Bohio (also called Quisqueya by the Taino), which he would name Hispaniola. (This is the island that's now home to Haiti and the Dominican Republic.) But Columbus's captains were getting frustrated and impatient. Martín Alonso Pinzón ditched Columbus and sailed ahead on the *Pinta* to look for gold on his own.

Columbus had the winds against him and had to go back to Cuba for wood and water, but eventually he made it to Hispaniola. When the local chief Guacanagari greeted him, Columbus was excited to see that Taino people were wearing gold ornaments there, too. Guacanagari even gave Columbus a gold-plated mask. Where was that gold coming from?

Columbus traveled east along the coast and ran into Pinzón, who said he'd been to a different part of the island where people were mining gold. They met various chiefs who gave them bits of gold, along with other gifts.

By then, the period Columbus had planned for his voyage was nearing its end. It was time to return to Spain, but there was a problem. The *Santa Maria* had

run aground on Christmas Eve. Columbus must have been kicking himself for not checking the depth in the bay to make sure it was safe. Instead, he'd taken his sailors' word for it, and apparently they didn't check all that well. The ship was totaled.

With the largest ship out of commission, there simply wasn't space on the others to get everyone back to Spain. Some of the crew members would have to stay and wait months for another ship to return and pick them up. As you can imagine, no one was excited about this.

But Columbus built a fort called La Navidad for the guys he was leaving behind and gave them supplies to last a year. Then he said goodbye, set sail with the *Niña* and the *Pinta,* and headed back to Spain.

FIVE

BACK AND FORTH ACROSS THE SEA

The return trip to Spain didn't go as smoothly as the original voyage. The winds weren't as favorable. The *Pinta* needed a new mast. (Columbus wondered in his writings why Martín Alonso Pinzón hadn't taken care of that instead of running off on his own to search for gold.) And they were low on food, too. All they had left was some bread, wine, and sweet potatoes, which must have gotten old after a while. They were saved by stacks of casabe gifted to them by their Taino hosts.

On Valentine's Day, Columbus got caught in a storm. Wind and waves tossed his ships all over the place. The *Pinta* was blown out of sight, and the *Niña* wasn't sailing well, either. Normally a ship has ballast, or weight, in the hold, which helps to steady it in the water. But Columbus had left so many of his supplies at La Navidad that there wasn't much left.

The crew filled some empty wine and water barrels with seawater, and that helped a little, but Columbus was still worried. What if he didn't make it back across the ocean? Historians believe Columbus was afraid that he might die *and* that Pinzón might live. What if the other captain sailed back to Spain alone and got all the credit? Just in case, Columbus wrote down the details of his voyage on parchment. He addressed it to the king and queen, wrapped it in waxed cloth, put it in a barrel, and threw the whole

thing overboard. Even if he didn't make it back to Spain, hopefully his words would.

That turned out to be unnecessary. On February 15, the crew spotted land. They'd sailed to the Azores. When the *Niña* landed on an island, there was a bit of a fight when the captain of that island arrested the men Columbus had sent ashore. Columbus was outraged. Didn't this guy know he was dealing with the Admiral of the Ocean Sea? Who did he think he was? Columbus threatened to sail to Spain and tell the king and queen how he was being treated.

The captain told him to go ahead and try that. He reminded Columbus that they were in Portuguese territory, where nobody cared what the Spanish monarchs had to say. Columbus was forced to leave without half his men. He returned a week later and was able to negotiate to get them back.

You might think that it would be smooth sailing after that, but on March 3, another storm almost ripped the sails off the *Niña*. A few days later, Columbus made it to the Rock of Sintra, near Lisbon. Still in Portuguese territory, he ended up having a meeting with the king of Portugal.

THE KING'S REGRETS?

There's a story about Columbus's meeting with the king of Portugal that involves the Taino men Columbus kidnapped and a container of dried beans. That account, from *History of the Indies* by Bartolomé de Las Casas, says the king asked one of the Taino men to arrange the beans in the form of the islands Columbus claimed to have visited on his trip. The man supposedly set up the beans to look like Cuba, the Bahamas, and Hispaniola. Then the king messed up the map and asked another Taino man to arrange the beans. His bean map verified the first map but with even more islands. The accuracy of Taino knowledge of the Caribbean backed up Columbus's claim. According to Las Casas, the king realized then what a mistake he'd made in not supporting Columbus's voyage and was furious with himself.

However, this story may need a little smashing.

OH, MAN OF POOR UNDERSTANDING, WHY DID YOU ALLOW SUCH AN ENTERPRISE OF SUCH IMPORTANCE TO GET OUT OF YOUR HANDS?

HMPH!

If you're thinking this sounds like the sort of story Columbus would tell to make himself feel big and important, you might be right. Historians doubt the king ever really said that, and his quote isn't mentioned in any of the other sources about the meeting.

The *Niña* and the *Pinta* made it back to Spain on March 15, and Columbus was ready to share his discoveries. He'd *meant* to find the lands Marco Polo described—the shining cities of gold and spices. Instead, he'd found a bunch of islands and accidentally started a colony on one of them when his ship got wrecked and he had to leave all those men behind. So he worked hard to put a positive spin on things.

Columbus was still insisting that he'd reached some part of Asia. That's why he called the people he met "Indians" and why the part of the world he explored is known as the West Indies today.

Columbus was still hoping to find the Asian ports he'd read about—the ones with all the spices and riches—but just in case it didn't work out, he wrote letters that made the Caribbean sound even *better* than where he'd meant to go. He said the islands were "fertile to limitless degree" with harbors "beyond comparison." He said Cuba was larger than England. (It's not; it's slightly larger than the state of Tennessee.) He said the lands were full of spices, gold, and other metals, even though he hadn't seen very much. And he announced that he'd founded a town "in the best position for the mines of gold . . . and for [trade] with the mainland." He left out the part about how he ended up there by accident after he wrecked his ship.

Even though Columbus's voyage hadn't gone the way he hoped, he was still confident and good at getting people to believe him. He quickly created a heroic public image for himself. People would crowd around when he passed through a town. When he arrived to see the king and queen, they held fancy dinners in his honor.

Columbus also benefited from the 1450 invention of the Gutenberg printing press, which made it much easier to spread news. His first "Letter to the Monarchs" of Spain, which described his trip, was printed all over Europe. He became a sensation within a few weeks after his return.

AN EGG-CELLENT TALE

There's a famous story about one of those dinners in Columbus's honor. It shows how he could work a crowd. According to a 1565 book written by Girolamo Benzoni, one of the guests claimed that Columbus's voyage wasn't really all that impressive; he said *anyone* could have crossed the sea and found those islands. In response, Columbus supposedly called for an egg and asked if anyone present could make it stand on end. Nobody could. Then Columbus stood the egg up himself, crushing down its shell just enough to form a flat base.

Columbus Breaking the Egg, engraving by William Hogarth, 1752

The moral of the story is that something looks impossible until someone figures out a way to do it, and then it looks easy. People liked that message, so they shared the story, and it became part of the Columbus legend—even though there's no real evidence that it's true. Benzoni wasn't at that dinner—he wasn't even born yet in 1493! Historians think Benzoni might have heard that story about the egg somewhere else and copied it, inserting Columbus as the hero.

Almost immediately, Columbus started making plans to go back to the Caribbean. He wanted more time to explore and set up a colony on Hispaniola. He'd also promised he'd be back for those men he left behind after the *Santa Maria* ran aground.

The king and queen of Spain supported a second voyage. Maybe Columbus hadn't reached Asia, but as long as he'd found new lands to exploit, they wanted him to make the most of it for Spain. They ordered him to set up gold mines, get some Spanish people settled in the islands, and establish trade with the Taino who lived there. The king and queen told Columbus to treat the Native people well and try to convert them to Christianity.

For this trip, they provided seventeen ships, more supplies, and more than a thousand men. Christopher Columbus's brother Diego was among them. (His brother Bartolomeo would join them in Hispaniola the following year.) The crew also included a doctor, a mapmaker, and a priest who was put in charge of learning about the Taino religion. Several of the Taino men Columbus had kidnapped were on the ships, too. One served as an interpreter for the second voyage.

THE SHIPS LEFT SPAIN ON SEPTEMBER 25, 1493.

THEY STOPPED IN THE CANARY ISLANDS TO PICK UP SUPPLIES. THIS TIME THEY BROUGHT PLANTS AND SOME LIVESTOCK TO ESTABLISH AGRICULTURE IN THE NEW COLONY.

THEN THEY HEADED ACROSS THE SEA TO HISPANIOLA, TO FIND THOSE CREW MEMBERS THEY'D LEFT BEHIND.

THEY ARRIVED IN THE CARIBBEAN IN EARLY NOVEMBER BUT GOT LOST ON THE ISLAND NOW CALLED GUADELOUPE FOR ALMOST A WEEK.

THEY ALSO EXPLORED THE SHORES OF WHAT ARE NOW THE VIRGIN ISLANDS AND PUERTO RICO.

AT THE END OF NOVEMBER, COLUMBUS MADE IT BACK TO THE PLACE WHERE THE SANTA MARIA HAD RUN AGROUND. BUT WHERE WERE THE SETTLERS HE'D LEFT BEHIND?

Columbus soon discovered that his men were dead and the fort was in ruins. While he was gone, some of his men had gotten sick. Others had spent their time stealing gold and supplies from Native people and attacking Native women, which led one of the strong chiefs, Caonabo, to declare war on them.

So much for that first settlement.

On top of that, some of Columbus's food had spoiled during the trip, so he had to ask the king and queen to send more supplies. He hadn't found all those Asian spices he was looking for, but he did find a bit of gold and some other spices, including those we now call chili peppers and allspice. So in early February, he sent one of his captains, Antonio de Torres, back to Spain with a dozen ships loaded with gold, spices, parrots, and Taino people they'd captured.

Because the colony wasn't doing well—they were still searching for all the riches—Columbus didn't have money to pay for food and other things he needed. So he suggested that the Spanish monarchs pay for his supplies by selling enslaved Native people.

Payment for these things could be made . . . in slaves . . . a people very savage and suitable for the purpose, and well made and of very good intelligence. We believe that they, having abandoned that inhumanity, will be better than any other slaves, and their inhumanity they will immediately lose when they are out of their own land.

In other words: "These people are both fierce and smart, and once we take them away from their homes, I'm sure they'll settle down and be good slaves."

(Kind of explains why Columbus's relationship with Native people of the islands wasn't going very well, doesn't it?)

Ferdinand and Isabella weren't impressed with any of this. First of all, Columbus had just gotten to the islands, so why was he already out of supplies? Also, they noticed that he'd mostly lost control of the soldiers they'd provided to help him. They sent word to Columbus that he needed to step up and take charge.

Queen Isabella also wasn't wild about the idea of enslaving her new subjects—at least not then. She told Columbus that it was fine for him to fight Native people if necessary, and that he should keep trying to convert them to Christianity but quit bringing them to Spain.

Meanwhile, Columbus was busy setting up a new town, which he named La Isabela, in honor of the queen. In March, he explored the Cibao Valley near La Isabela, searching for gold, and built a fort called Santo Tomás to protect his men there.

Then Columbus set out exploring again. He left his brother Diego in charge and took off with the *Niña,* along with two smaller boats, to explore the coast of Cuba (which Columbus still thought was attached to Asia). Then they headed for what is now Jamaica when someone told Columbus he might find gold there. (He still *really* wanted gold.) But once again, he came up empty and decided that Hispaniola probably offered his best chance at striking it rich.

By then it was September, and Columbus had to

ride out a hurricane before returning to La Isabela. He also wasn't feeling well. When he finally got back, he was so sick he had to be carried to shore.

And that was just the beginning of his problems. A lot had happened while he was gone.

Before Columbus took off for Cuba, he'd ordered one of his captains, Pedro Margarit, to take four hundred men into the interior of Hispaniola to find the Indian gold mines. Margarit's mission found a little gold but not much. They also didn't find much food. They went back to La Isabela hungry, only to discover that there wasn't enough food in the settlement, either. The men who'd stayed were mad about being left behind and hadn't taken care of the gardens. Fed up with the whole situation, Margarit took off with three ships and hightailed it back to Spain.

The La Isabela colonists who remained were still hungry, so they raided the Taino people's storehouses and stole their food. The Taino were understandably upset about that and fought back, and when Columbus returned, he found that his remaining men were in the middle of a war with the people they were supposed to be trading with.

The Taino people didn't have the metal swords and guns the Spanish did (or the cannons, war-horses, or attack dogs), but they were fierce fighters nonetheless. They threw gourds full of ashes and hot ground peppers at the Spanish and then, wearing cloths over their faces for protection, charged through and attacked with wooden swords, spears, stones, and slings. When they had to retreat, they destroyed their homes and gardens, denying the Spanish any of their food. The battles dragged on and on, but one by one, the Taino caciques and their main warriors fell to Spanish war weapons.

Meanwhile, Columbus was still trying to convince people back in Spain that everything was going just swell. You might think, since the queen told him to stop capturing Taino people, that he'd knock it off and quit doing that. But he was desperate to prove that the colony could make money, so in February 1495, he used a Taino attack on the Spanish settlement as justification to round up another 1,600 adults and children to be sent to Europe and sold as slaves. When he could fit only a third of them on the ships, he kept many as laborers and let the rest go.

As you can imagine, this made relations with the

Taino people even worse. By 1496, Columbus was also enslaving Taino men to work for the settlers. And on top of all that, germs that the Spanish had brought from Europe were deadly to the Taino people.

Back in Europe, people were buzzing about everything Columbus was doing wrong. Things in the settlement had gotten so bad that more of Columbus's own men bailed on him, setting off in ships to go home and telling everyone what a mess he'd made.

Maybe you're thinking this is where Ferdinand and Isabella decided enough was enough. Time to call it quits on this whole adventure, right?

Nope. To help Columbus out, they sent more livestock and recruited people who knew how to farm and build things. They also sent one of their royal household officials, Juan Aguado, to investigate Columbus and his brother Diego. Were all those rumors true? Was Columbus really doing as bad a job as people said?

Aguado made the trip and reported back that the answer was yes. Columbus had made a mess of things. Native people were dying, and so were colonists. Those who survived kept leaving and sailing home to Spain.

In April 1496, Columbus left his brother Bartolomeo in charge of the settlement and sailed back to Spain, too. He arrived on June 11. And boy, did he have some explaining to do.

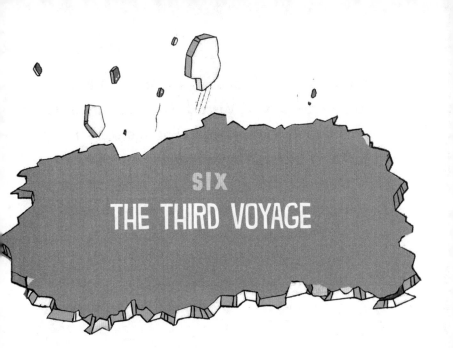

SIX
THE THIRD VOYAGE

By the time Columbus got back to Spain, the king and queen had come to understand a few things. They realized that Columbus wasn't great at managing people and that there weren't going to be immediate riches pouring out of these islands he'd found. You might be thinking that at this point, they'd cut their losses and tell Columbus he was on his own. But believe it or not, they decided to send him on yet another voyage.

Why would they do that when none of his promises about heaps of gold and spices and routes to Asia were coming true? The reason probably has to do with competition from other nations. Portugal was getting ready to send Vasco da Gama out to look for a new sea route to India, and England was sending John Cabot to search for a northern route to Asia.

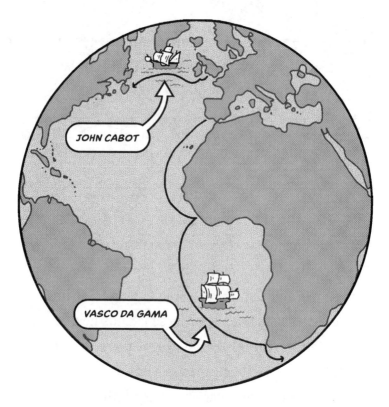

Spain didn't want to be left out, and the monarchs figured Columbus was probably their best bet, so they stuck with him. Columbus was still insisting he'd reached some unknown part of Asia (though not many people believed him anymore), and he wanted to keep exploring. But he'd also turned his attention to colonizing the islands he did find and exploiting their natural resources and people.

The Spanish monarchs were ready for Columbus to pick up where he'd left off at the end of his last voyage. But the truth is, things in the islands had grown even more complicated while he was away.

Before he left, Columbus had started a policy that required Taino people to pay tributes to the Spanish in order to live on the islands where they'd lived all their lives.

. . . on all those living near the mines, everyone from fourteen years up, each three months . . . a Flemish hawk's bell . . . full of gold.

We're not exactly sure how much gold fit in a hawk's bell, which was a small bell used in falconry and as a trade item. The largest were about an inch and a half in diameter, about the size of a golf ball. But even smaller bells would have been a problem because there just wasn't that much gold on Hispaniola. What the Spanish had first seen as abundance was actually gold that Taino people had collected over many generations. So the Spanish sometimes took other tributes, forcing Taino people to bring cotton, spices, or food instead. But gold was the main obsession, and the colonizers sometimes cut off Taino people's fingers or hands as punishment for not providing it.

Even so, the quotas were pretty much impossible to meet. Just before Columbus left to go back to Spain, his men had found gold in another area of the island, so while he was gone, his brother Bartolomeo had shifted his attention there. He set up a new port called Santo Domingo and started taking supplies and equipment there from La Isabela.

That made it harder for the La Isabela settlers to collect their tributes, and they weren't happy about the mess Bartolomeo had made. Francisco Roldán, who'd been left in charge of La Isabela, staged a revolt. He got local Taino to help by promising that if he gained control, he would end the tribute system.

That didn't work out very well for the Taino. Bartolomeo captured two caciques along with other Taino people, and shipped them to Europe to be enslaved. He couldn't defeat Roldán, though, so the whole situation was still unsettled when Ferdinand and Isabella started making plans to send Columbus back for his third voyage.

In July 1497, the king and queen issued their orders for that next trip. They gave Columbus permission to appoint more administrators for the colonies. They arranged for soldiers, sailors, mine workers, and farmers to go, too. And for the first time, they decided to send some women—a sign that they were looking to establish a more permanent settlement. The ships were also loaded with oxen, horses, donkeys, and supplies for farming and mining.

The king and queen told Columbus it was fine for him to keep demanding tributes. They suggested that each Taino person wear some sort of necklace with a brass or lead coin that could be marked to keep track of payments. The monarchs also allowed Columbus

to give land to colonists who promised to live in the islands for at least fourteen years. (Not surprisingly, no one consulted with the Taino people, who'd lived on that land for generations.)

The king and queen gave Columbus fourteen ships. Eight were loaded early and went ahead of the others. The next three ships were earmarked for Columbus to use for more exploration once he got to the Caribbean. The last three were meant to carry supplies and up to three hundred more colonists . . . *if* they could find anyone who wanted to go. Most people didn't, so once again the king and queen offered a deal to prisoners and picked up another ten murderers turned sailors.

The voyage was delayed over and over, and Columbus was getting pretty stressed. He lashed out at an official in Seville who'd been talking trash about his West Indies explorations, kicking the guy and pulling his hair.

The trip finally got underway in May 1498. Three supply ships went straight to Hispaniola while Columbus took his ships a little farther south to explore. By now, you can probably guess that he was hoping to find gold, and you can also probably guess that he didn't.

He did, however, find the island we now call Trinidad and went on to see the mountains of what is now Venezuela, in South America. When he reached the mouth of the Orinoco River, he was convinced that he'd located an earthly paradise he'd read about in the Bible—the source of the Ganges, Tigris, Euphrates, and Nile Rivers, all rolled into one magical place. He was pretty psyched about that.

For I have never read or heard of so great a quantity of fresh water so coming into and near the salt. . . . And if it does not come from there, from paradise, it seems to be a still greater marvel, for I do not believe that there is known in the world a river so great and so deep.

Columbus and his men had also found some pearl oyster beds off the coast of Venezuela, so they were in a great mood when they headed back to Hispaniola. But that changed the second they arrived.

The colonists had mutinied! They were openly rebelling against Spanish officials. The Taino people were also fed up with the colonists and their stupid tributes. Columbus's brothers Bartolomeo and Diego had totally lost control. That Roldán guy and his supporters were still staging their revolt, and other colonists just wanted to get out of there. Columbus sent them home and, still ignoring the queen's orders to quit capturing Taino men, let each one take an enslaved Taino person along with them.

All the while, Columbus was writing letters back to Spain, telling the king and queen to ignore all those people saying bad things about him because everything was going great. But now the royals knew that wasn't true. How great could things be if there was an uprising? Also, why did Columbus keep sending enslaved Taino people to Spain when they'd specifically told him to knock it off?

When Columbus had first started having trouble

with Roldán, he'd asked the Spanish monarchs to investigate, and they'd sent a man named Francisco de Bobadilla to do that. Now they decided it was time to give Bobadilla even more power to investigate the situation and try to restore order to the colony.

Ferdinand and Isabella were clearly losing faith in Columbus. They'd promised him rights to explore that whole region but broke their promise and approved other explorers' voyages. Among them was Amerigo Vespucci, who in 1501 would explore the southern coast of what is now South America. He came to the conclusion that it wasn't Asia at all but

Amerigo Vespucci

an entirely different landmass. He'd end up getting his name on not one but two continents.

Meanwhile, Columbus was trying to manage hundreds of settlers and struggling to work things out with the still-revolting Roldán. Columbus continued to ignore the queen's rules about how to treat the Taino and gave Roldán the right to force Native people to work for him. He said it was fine for Roldán to move the islanders around wherever he wanted and have them do whatever work he pleased.

That satisfied Roldán, so he finally settled down, but by then smaller uprisings were breaking out in the countryside. Columbus sent some of the rebels back to Santo Domingo to be punished. When Bobadilla arrived from Spain to restore order, he saw some of those men hanging from the gallows on shore as his ship approached. It must have made a great first impression.

Obviously, things weren't going well on the island. As soon as Bobadilla landed, he seized control, arrested Diego, and demanded that Columbus surrender, too. In October 1500, both Diego and Christopher Columbus boarded a ship in chains to be sent back to Spain.

On the ship, Columbus wrote a letter to a friend, knowing the queen would end up seeing it.

Most Virtuous Lady: If it is something new for me to complain of the world, its custom of mistreating me is very old standing. A thousand battles have I fought with it, and I have withstood all until now when neither arms nor wit avail me. With cruelty, it has cast me down to the depth. . . . I gave with such earnest love to serve these princes, and I have served with a service that has never been heard or seen.

In other words: "I've done everything for these people, and look how they're treating me!"

Columbus spent six weeks in jail, but eventually, the king and queen ordered him released. They let him keep some of his titles and all of his property but banned him from setting foot on Hispaniola ever again.

So that was the end of Columbus's explorations, right?

Wrong. There was still one more voyage to go.

SEVEN
ONE LAST TRIP

Before Columbus set out on his fourth voyage, Spain sent a new governor to be in charge of Hispaniola. In February 1502, Nicolás de Ovando left for the Caribbean with thirty-two ships and 2,500 settlers and sailors—more than Columbus had ever been given for one of his voyages.

Ovando was crueler to the Taino people than Columbus was, but he seemed better suited to the job of managing the Spanish colony. If the monarchs had learned anything from Columbus, it was that the skills a person needed to go exploring weren't necessarily the same skills that would help them run a settlement.

Spain also appointed more officials to help manage the islands—overseers and workers to process the gold being mined, along with a chief justice and a treasurer. The Spanish got permission from the

Nicolás de Ovando

church to collect tithes, a sort of tax to support the church and clergy in the islands. And they made more rules for the Native people, banning them from having any European weapons. They were beginning to lay the groundwork for a Spanish Empire across the sea.

Those plans were all in motion by the time Columbus set out on his fourth voyage in May 1502, ready to explore the area between Cuba and northeastern South America. By then, his son Hernando was thirteen years old and went along, too. There were four boats with a total of 135 people. Most were young and inexperienced; just 43 were over the age of eighteen.

If you're wondering why Columbus decided to make that fourth voyage with a bunch of teenagers, it's because he didn't have much of a choice. Historians believe that by then, many of the better sailors were busy with their own voyages, and others just didn't want to go with Columbus, given his history.

But the trip went smoothly—Hernando would later write that they crossed the ocean "without having to touch the sails"—and they reached the island of Matinino (now called Martinique) on June 15. From there, Columbus sailed through the Antilles and reached Hispaniola on June 29.

You're probably thinking, "Hey, wait a minute! Didn't the king and queen specifically tell him *not* to go there?" They did. But by now you know that Columbus wasn't great about following orders. Besides, one of his ships, the *Santiago*, wasn't doing that well, and he was hoping to sell it and get another one.

As Columbus was arriving in Hispaniola, Ovando was about to send a fleet of ships back to Spain. And a hurricane was approaching, too.

Anchored offshore, Columbus sent a message to Ovando, warning him about the nasty weather on the way and suggesting that maybe he shouldn't send his ships out into the storm. Columbus also asked for permission to use the harbor to shelter his own ships. Ovando ignored the warning, refused Columbus's request to land, and ordered his own fleet to head out as planned.

Columbus had been wrong about a lot of things, but this time, he was right. Twenty-five of Ovando's ships sank in the storm. Only three or four survived.

After waiting out the hurricane, Columbus explored the coast of Central America, including islands off the coast of Honduras. There, he saw a very large canoe made of a single tree trunk. It was eight feet wide, with twenty-five people paddling it, and had a pavilion in the middle and a roof made of palm tree fronds with women, children, baggage, and all kinds of supplies underneath. The goods included cotton clothing, wooden swords, sharp flint knives, and copper hatchets as well as copper bells and crucibles for melting metal. It was impressive, so you might think Columbus would change course and sail to explore the place these people had come from.

Nope. Because Columbus was *still* holding on to the idea that he'd made it to an unknown region of Asia. He was hoping that he'd soon find a passage to the part with all the nice cities and spices and gold. So he kept sailing south. He claimed the South American mainland for Spain (by now, you know he wasn't worried about the people who had lived there for thousands of years before he showed up) and explored the coast of Panama. Columbus wasn't the first European to see Panama; Rodrigo de Bastidas had searched for gold along the coast in 1501. But Columbus hoped he might find a strait leading to what he thought would be the rest of Asia.

If Columbus *had* found a water route through Panama, he would have ended up in the Pacific Ocean and, if he'd kept going a really long way, eventually Asia. But there was no water passage then. It wouldn't exist for another four hundred years, when the Panama Canal was completed in 1914.

Since that didn't work out, Columbus tried to establish a settlement on a river they named Río Belén, or River of Bethlehem. His plan was to leave Bartolomeo with one of the ships, break it up, and use the lumber for buildings. But Native people who lived there fought back. Spanish documents don't specify which tribal nation was engaging with Columbus, but we know that the Kuna, Choco, and Guaymi people lived in what is now Panama at that time. They were all skilled at pottery making, stonecutting, and working with metal and would have been able to defend themselves well. Eventually Columbus gave up, left the remains of that ship behind, and started back to Spain.

Columbus and his crew had already abandoned another vessel because it was damaged by shipworms, so now they were down to two ships. The trip back to Spain was anything but smooth sailing.

MAY 1, 1503

COLUMBUS'S REMAINING SHIPS WERE RIDDLED WITH WORM HOLES. SAILORS PUMPED AND BAILED WATER AROUND THE CLOCK TO KEEP THE VESSELS AFLOAT.

THEY WERE ALSO RUNNING LOW ON FOOD.

SMASH!

ONE NIGHT, THE SHIPS COLLIDED DURING A STORM.

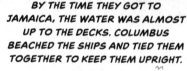

THERE WAS TOO MUCH DAMAGE. THEY'D NEVER MAKE IT BACK TO SPAIN.

BY THE TIME THEY GOT TO JAMAICA, THE WATER WAS ALMOST UP TO THE DECKS. COLUMBUS BEACHED THE SHIPS AND TIED THEM TOGETHER TO KEEP THEM UPRIGHT.

THE MEN BUILT CABINS ON THE DECKS SO THEY COULD LIVE ON BOARD UNTIL SOMEBODY CAME TO RESCUE THEM.

THEY WAITED . . .

. . . AND WAITED.

FINALLY, THE SPANISH MEN DECIDED THEY'D TRY TO SEND A GROUP TO HISPANIOLA IN NATIVE PEOPLE'S CANOES TO GET HELP.

COLUMBUS AND THE REST OF HIS CREW JUST KEPT WAITING.

While Columbus was stranded, he wrote a rambling letter to the Spanish monarchs, letting them know just how badly he thought he was being treated and asking for all his titles and honors to be restored. He told them that while he was waiting to be rescued, he'd had a vision that God chose him to find the Indies and totally wanted him to have those islands. He said he was sure God had been watching him ever since he was born.

This voice Columbus said he heard also compared him to heroes from the Bible and said his best times were yet to come. Columbus wrapped up his letter by admitting he wasn't certain whose voice he'd heard. Still, he vowed to keep trying to conquer other lands for Christianity because he was sure that was what God wanted.

Since Columbus was stranded, there was no immediate way for him to send his letter. But that didn't really matter. When Ferdinand and Isabella did finally get to read it, they just ignored it anyway.

SIGH

AFTER MONTHS OF WAITING TO BE RESCUED, COLUMBUS'S MEN WERE OUT OF PATIENCE.

THE ARAWAK PEOPLE WHO LIVED ON THE ISLAND WERE TIRED OF DEALING WITH THE SPANISH. THEY'D BEEN TRADING WITH THEM FOR MONTHS, AND THEIR OWN FOOD SUPPLIES WERE RUNNING LOW.

COLUMBUS WAS DESPERATE, SO HE TOLD A WHOPPER OF A LIE TO GET WHAT HE WANTED.

HE KNEW FROM HIS NAVIGATION AND ASTRONOMY TABLES THAT THERE WOULD SOON BE A LUNAR ECLIPSE.

MARCH 1, 1504

SO HE ARRANGED TO MEET WITH LOCAL LEADERS THE DAY BEFORE IT HAPPENED.

COLUMBUS TOLD THE ARAWAK MEN THAT GOD WAS MAD AT THEM FOR CHARGING HIM TOO MUCH FOR FOOD AND WOULD SOON SEND A SIGN OF HIS ANGER. HE TOLD THE MEN TO WATCH THE MOON THAT NIGHT.

SURE ENOUGH . . .

ACCORDING TO HERNANDO'S LATER WRITINGS, THE ARAWAK PEOPLE CAME BACK TO THE SHIPS WITH OFFERS OF FOOD, EVEN ASKING COLUMBUS TO TALK WITH HIS GOD FOR THEM.

The Admiral replied that he wished to speak briefly with his God, and retired to his cabin while the eclipse waxed and the Indians cried all the time for his help.

COLUMBUS WAITED IN HIS CABIN UNTIL THE ECLIPSE WAS ALMOST OVER. THEN HE CAME OUT AND SAID HE'D FIXED EVERYTHING—BY PROMISING GOD THAT THE ARAWAK WOULD TREAT THE SPANISH WELL AND BRING THEM WHATEVER THEY NEEDED.

ACCORDING TO HERNANDO, THE SPANISH MEN GOT THEIR FOOD AFTER THAT. BUT REMEMBER: HIS STORIES MADE HIS DAD LOOK GOOD. WE DON'T HAVE THE ARAWAK VERSION OF THIS EVENT!

124

Eight months after that group set out for Hispaniola, a Spanish ship arrived in Jamaica. Finally! Columbus and his men were being rescued. Right?

Wrong. The crew dropped off some pork and wine but said sorry, they didn't have a ship big enough to rescue the men, so Columbus would have to keep waiting. Eventually, a rescue ship did arrive, and they all sailed to Santo Domingo, on Hispaniola.

It was fall of 1504 when Columbus finally sailed back to Spain. Most of his crew stayed behind; only some family and close friends went with him. And the trip wasn't great. Soon after they set out, one of the mainmasts split, so they had to jerry-rig a new one, and they lost another mast in a storm along the way. They were lucky to make it back to Spain on November 7, 1504.

Columbus wanted to meet with the king and queen to report on his voyage, but he didn't get to do that. The queen had been sick, and she died soon after Columbus returned.

The truth is, Columbus wasn't feeling all that well himself. He was pretty sick by the time he arrived back in Spain, and he died less than two years later. Even though some people had figured out that Columbus never made it to Asia, he died insisting that he had. Columbus has come down in history as a "grand discoverer" of the Americas, a hero to many; but for many others, he is a symbol of the beginning of a terrible destruction.

THE TOMBS OF CHRISTOPHER COLUMBUS?

If you ever want to visit the final resting place of Christopher Columbus, you'll have a decision to make. Both Spain and the Dominican Republic claim to have his remains.

Columbus was originally buried in Spain, but his family asked that his remains and those of his son Diego be sent to Hispaniola and interred in the cathedral there. When the French captured that island in 1795, the Spanish quickly dug up the remains they believed to be Christopher Columbus and hurried them off to Cuba. In 1898, those remains were sent to Spain.

The tomb of Christopher Columbus at the Seville Cathedral in Spain

The Columbus tomb at Columbus Lighthouse in Santo Domingo, Dominican Republic

But back in 1877, somebody found a box full of human remains in the Hispaniola cathedral, and it had Columbus's name on it.

Did that mean Christopher Columbus never got moved after all? Did the bones in the box belong to his son? Or did the explorer's remains get split into two different batches, now with an ocean between them?

In 2006, DNA testing showed that at least some of the remains in Spain belong to Columbus. The other box of bones is now in the Columbus Lighthouse in Santo Domingo, in the Dominican Republic. The lighthouse director insists that he's the guy watching over Columbus's final resting place, but the Dominican Republic won't allow the bones to be tested (they say it's disrespectful to the dead), so no one knows for sure if Columbus is buried in Spain, the Dominican Republic, or a little of both.

EIGHT

WHAT HAPPENED NEXT

Before Columbus died, he'd set in motion the events that would lead to colonization of the Americas. That meant riches for the nations of Europe and devastation for the Taino and other Native people.

When Nicolás de Ovando took over the settlement on Hispaniola in 1502, he wouldn't tolerate any Taino chiefs still having authority over their own lands. Ovando figured it threatened the settlers he'd brought along, and their need for land. So he started killing the chiefs. In the fall of 1503, he visited the chiefdom of Xaragua, where the now-legendary woman cacique Anacaona welcomed him and called the other chiefs to meet with him. While they were all gathered, Ovando ordered his soldiers to block the door and burn down the building with the Taino leaders trapped inside.

Ovando also expanded the enslavement of Taino people, with what the Spanish called the encomienda system. Under this system, Taino people were forced to work for the Spanish for six months or more before being released back to their villages so they could grow cassava and recover from the brutal work in the mines. Six months was to be the working period, but often it stretched to nearly a year.

Many Taino got sick. Working conditions were awful, and people weren't given enough time to hunt, fish, and grow food so they could eat well. Between that and the diseases spread by European settlers, the Taino population plummeted. Meanwhile, the Spanish population was growing. They set up more towns around Hispaniola and expanded to what is now called Puerto Rico.

In 1509, Christopher Columbus's son Diego took over for Ovando as viceroy, or ruler, of the islands.

He conquered Jamaica, and another Spanish explorer named Diego Velázquez de Cuéllar arrived to conquer Cuba in 1511.

Diego Columbus   Diego Velázquez de Cuéllar

Meanwhile, so many Taino people were dying in the gold mines that the Spanish were growing worried. It wasn't that they cared about the Taino; they were concerned because all those deaths led to a shortage of workers, especially since many other Native people were moving to isolated places. By 1515, the Spanish were capturing and enslaving people across the islands.

A SOLUTION TO NATIVE SLAVERY?

You might be reading about all this enslavement of Taino people and wondering what happened to Queen Isabella's orders. Hadn't she declared Native people to be her royal subjects? Didn't she tell those explorers to quit enslaving people?

The answer is yes ... sort of. Spain's original policy was that Native people should not be enslaved. But within a few years, that policy began to change. The queen declared that slavery was okay as long as the people being enslaved had been captured in what she called a "just war." Conveniently, the Spanish definition of a "just war" included most any conflict with Native or non-Christian people.

In 1512, the Spanish government issued the Laws of Burgos, which outlined a fairer treatment for Native people in the colonies.

It seemed like a step in the right direction, but it turned out that the laws were nearly impossible to enforce from all the way across the ocean.

Bartolomé de Las Casas was a Spanish settler who arrived in the Caribbean with Ovando in 1502. He went on to become a priest and an outspoken advocate for Native people in the islands. He wrote a whole book about how they were being treated and had harsh words for his fellow Spaniards.

The Spaniards first set Sail to America, not for the Honor of God, or as Persons moved and merited thereunto by servant Zeal to the True Faith, nor to promote the Salvation of their Neighbours, nor to serve the King, as they falsely boast and pretend to do, but in truth, only stimulated and goaded on by insatiable Avarice and Ambition, that they might for ever Domineer, Command, and Tyrannize over the West-Indians, whose Kingdoms they hoped to divide and distribute among themselves.

In other words: These Spanish explorers weren't really aiming to spread Christianity or do good work in the world. They were settlers looking for land and riches, and many were mean, greedy people who would be brutal in their quest for money and power.

But before you start cheering for Las Casas, there's something else you should know about him. At first, in looking for a solution to the poor treatment of Native people, he suggested that the Spanish start enslaving African people to work in the islands instead. (Later, he regretted his words and said it was also wrong to enslave African people. But it took him a while.)

By 1520, the Spanish had cleared out nearly all the gold in Hispaniola, Puerto Rico, and Cuba. Most of the Taino people had died working in the gold mines or from smallpox and other diseases the Spanish brought with them from Europe.

With the gold depleted, the Spanish forced the remaining enslaved Taino people to raise animals and grow sugarcane instead. Then they brought more enslaved workers from other parts of the Caribbean, and soon from Africa as well.

Columbus's voyages began what would be a major and sustained blow to the Native peoples of the Americas. In 1491, the Inca Empire had been the largest on earth, stretching from the Amazon rain forest to the Andes to the coast of what is now Peru. The Aztec Empire had a population of more than five million people living in what is now Mexico.

Within a hundred years, Spanish explorers—and the diseases they brought with them—would destroy both of these empires, along with hundreds of smaller nations. Over the centuries, other European countries, such as Holland, France, and England, also conquered peoples and territories in the Americas.

The whole thing was set in motion by a man who died without ever figuring out that he hadn't sailed

Ferdinand Magellan

to Asia. It would be more than a decade before Ferdinand Magellan's crew circumnavigated the globe—sailed all the way around it—and people learned just how long a journey it actually was. Only then did they understand the true size of the earth—and how far off the mark Columbus had been.

So if Columbus didn't find Asia and didn't sail around the world, what did he actually accomplish?

The truth is, even though he never found what he was looking for, his explorations did open up new trade routes for the people of Europe. By the time of his second voyage, goods were being shipped back and forth across the Atlantic, and this eventually led to global trading. In that sense, his voyages did change the world.

THE COLUMBIAN EXCHANGE

All those trips back and forth across the sea created what is now called the Columbian Exchange—the introduction of plants, animals, and ideas between Europe, Asia, Africa, and the Americas. Not all of the exchanges were positive. The new food crops were great. The cockroaches and diseases? Not so much.

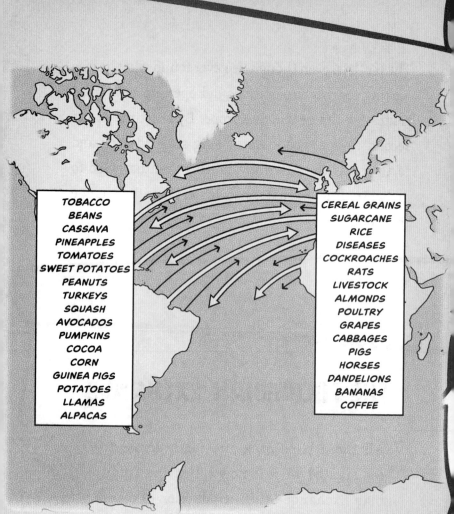

TOBACCO
BEANS
CASSAVA
PINEAPPLES
TOMATOES
SWEET POTATOES
PEANUTS
TURKEYS
SQUASH
AVOCADOS
PUMPKINS
COCOA
CORN
GUINEA PIGS
POTATOES
LLAMAS
ALPACAS

CEREAL GRAINS
SUGARCANE
RICE
DISEASES
COCKROACHES
RATS
LIVESTOCK
ALMONDS
POULTRY
GRAPES
CABBAGES
PIGS
HORSES
DANDELIONS
BANANAS
COFFEE

Sometimes, early settlers didn't understand what would happen with those newly
introduced plants and animals. They soon
learned that European pigs, for example,

didn't have natural predators in America, so the eight from Columbus's second voyage reproduced like wildfire. Bartolomé de Las Casas would later write, "From those eight sows have multiplied all the pigs which until today have been and are in the Indies, which have been and are infinite."

Infinite pigs!

(Maybe he exaggerated a little, but they did end up with a lot of pigs.)

NINE

THE TAINO PEOPLE TODAY

Over fifty years of war, slavery, and disease, the Taino people were nearly destroyed. In 1542, Spain enacted the New Laws, meant to abolish slavery of Native people of the Americas. Bartolomé de Las Casas led the campaign for these new laws. But so much damage was already done.

There was a massive population decline after the Spanish showed up. For Taino people, it was a time of pure terror. It has been said that Taino even became extinct, but this is another myth that needs to be smashed.

Taino people survived.

It's true that their natural way of life was drastically changed. But historians estimate that about one in ten Taino people survived that period of conquest. Some escaped to the mountains and formed rebel camps. On the island of Hispaniola, the cacique Enriquillo resisted Spanish rule. He took his people to the mountains, where they spent fourteen years fighting for a treaty from the Spanish. They eventually won and were guaranteed their own territory.

A statue of Enriquillo in the Dominican Republic

In Cuba and Puerto Rico, most Taino people were enslaved. But many also rebelled. They escaped and formed communities, called palenques, from which they raided the Spanish farms and attacked colonial troops. After fifty years of suffering and fighting, the Taino people won their liberty from slavery. Many of those who survived settled in pueblos de Indios, or Indian towns. Others lived near the Spanish towns, becoming border guards, cowboys, road construction workers, and teachers. Taino herbalists and healers counted Spanish settlers among their patients.

The surviving generation of Taino, known simply as Indios, adjusted as best they could. They survived by adapting and resisting, and by isolating themselves deeper into the forested mountains and remote ocean coves. Many Taino men had been killed in the fighting and as a result of cruel treatment while they worked in the gold mines.

Though Taino women were also treated brutally by the conquerors, more of them survived. Some married men who had come from Spain or men who had been brought from Africa in the slave trade. These changing Taino families, some of full heritage and others blended, identified as Indios, or naturales.

The Barrientos family of Cuba, headed by an Indigenous woman from Baracoa and a former Spanish soldier, 1919

These families maintained many traditional customs. They passed down generations' worth of knowledge about natural medicines and healing and taught their traditional farming techniques to their children. Their many Native food plants, such as corn, beans, tomatoes, peppers, manioc, sweet yams, and various fruits, became the foods of the new, more blended population.

The small farmers of the Caribbean islands inherited much of this resilient Taino knowledge and natural farming lifestyle, which now incorporates animals and plants from Europe, Africa, and Asia. Over time, the farming families most related to this Taino legacy became known as guajiros in Cuba and parts of the Dominican Republic, as jibaros in Puerto Rico, and as Maroons in Jamaica and other islands. In the smaller islands, like St. Vincent, Dominica, and Trinidad and Tobago, the Taino ancestry now blends into the Garifuna, and into the Kalinago, or Carib, peoples.

The Taino were labeled as "extinct" in history books for many years, but new studies of the genetics of people in the Caribbean islands have confirmed high percentages of Taino or American Indian ancestry. Many Caribbean families of Taino heritage have come forward more publicly and are reunifying as Taino. Various groups are dedicated to the preservation and recovery of the Taino language, herbal knowledge, music, song, dance, featherwork, basketry, pottery, and other arts. The United Confederation of Taino People and other Taino organizations participate in the United Nations Permanent Forum on Indigenous Issues.

The most well-known living group of Caribbean Indios is in the eastern mountains of Cuba. They are La Gran Familia India de Cuba, with more than twenty rural and urban communities and at least fifteen thousand of their own kinship people. They uphold the authority of a traditional cacique, who has stepped forward with the elder women's circle and the younger leaders to educate other Cubans and the world about their existence.

They all say, "Taino is here to stay, because Taino is alive."

Cacique Francisco Ramírez Rojas, Native community of La Rancheria, Guantánamo Province, Cuba, with his wife, abuela Reina, and four daughters, 2016

TEN
THE LEGACY OF CHRISTOPHER COLUMBUS

After all this discussion of Columbus and the Taino people, you might be wondering how Columbus got to be such a big deal. After all, the Spanish monarchs were so unhappy with him that they basically fired him and sent somebody else to run the colony. So how did he end up with a national holiday? The truth is, it took centuries.

After Columbus died, he was largely forgotten. There were no big celebrations on the one hundredth anniversary of his first voyage.

Or the two hundredth anniversary.

But by the late 1700s, Columbus was becoming more popular in the United States.

"Columbia, America as sometimes so called from Columbus, the first discoverer."

—AMERICAN POET PHILIP FRENEAU, 1777

Some people argued that the United States should be named after Columbus. They didn't win that argument—the Americas were named after Amerigo Vespucci—but the name Columbus started popping up all over the place. In 1791, the new United States capital was named the territory of Columbia. (Today, it's called Washington, DC, which stands for "District of Columbia.") King's College in New York

City was renamed Columbia in 1784, and South Carolina named its state capital after the explorer, too. The song "Hail, Columbia" became America's unofficial national anthem.

"*Hail, Columbia, happy land!*"

Why the sudden interest in an explorer who'd been dead for well over two centuries? It doesn't seem to make sense—until you consider the timing. America had just won its independence from Great Britain in the Revolutionary War, and people were searching for a symbol of their history that didn't revolve around the nation they'd just spent years fighting. Columbus wasn't British; he'd been born in Genoa. Many Americans saw honoring him as a way to honor their history without giving Britain all the credit, and they cheerfully ignored the fact that

Columbus never actually set foot in what is now the United States.

Early American textbooks featured Columbus in the first chapter and mostly erased Native people. This can also be explained by looking at what was happening in the country at that time. The United States wanted to expand its territory, which meant taking even more Native land. The last thing its leaders wanted to do was remind everyone that Native people had been there first.

Columbus got even more attention in 1828, when Washington Irving wrote a fictionalized biography of the explorer that painted him as a true American hero. Some school textbooks used that book as a source, even though much of it was made up or exaggerated.

So when did people start questioning that glorified version of Columbus's life story? Around the four hundredth anniversary of Columbus's first voyage, there was a big celebration held in Chicago, and a number of writers published new research about his life around that time. One of them, Justin Winsor, started asking questions about whether Columbus was really as heroic as Irving's book made him out to be.

Winsor had noticed, based on historical documents, that Columbus was a bold navigator and a good salesman for his own ideas, but he wasn't great at following directions. He'd broken a bunch of the Spanish monarchs' rules, gotten into all kinds of conflicts with Native people, and essentially tried to set up the first transatlantic slave trade. So maybe he wasn't such a great guy after all.

That information all came out before 1900, but most American textbooks stuck with the old version of the Columbus story, choosing to show the explorer as a role model—someone who could inspire kids! Those other details didn't fit that narrative, so they were most often left out.

So how did Columbus end up getting his own American holiday when he never even landed in what is now the United States?

If America wanted to honor explorers, why not set aside a day to celebrate Ponce de León, who landed in Florida in 1513? What about Giovanni da Verrazzano, who sailed into New York Harbor in 1524? (He got a bridge named after him, but no holiday.)

The answer to this Columbus question also has to do with history and timing. In the 1820s, more

Italian Americans were immigrating to the United States. They had darker skin than people whose ancestors had come from England, and they were Catholic instead of Protestant. Because of that, they had to deal with a lot of discrimination, just as many immigrants face prejudice in the United States today. In the 1800s, Italian Americans were sometimes targets of violent attacks.

In 1891, a mob broke into a New Orleans jail and lynched eleven Italian immigrants after nine of

them had been accused of killing the city police commissioner. The men had already stood trial—six had been found not guilty, and a mistrial was declared for the other three—but that didn't stop the angry crowd from murdering them, along with two other Italian men who had nothing to do with any of it. The killings were fueled by prejudice and hatred.

It was a huge problem, and some people decided that the way to solve it was to lift up a hero from Italy. They chose Christopher Columbus and asked the United States to set aside a day to honor him. Italian Americans who'd been fighting discrimination hoped that a nation honoring Columbus would realize that people from Italy (or the land that would one day become Italy, anyway) deserved respect and acceptance.

In 1892, President Benjamin Harrison called for a national observance of Columbus Day. That helped him gain support from Italian American voters and also helped smooth things over with Italy, where leaders were still understandably upset about what had happened in New Orleans.

ON THAT DAY LET THE PEOPLE, SO FAR AS POSSIBLE, CEASE FROM ALL TOIL AND DEVOTE THEMSELVES TO SUCH EXERCISES AS MAY BEST EXPRESS HONOR TO THE DISCOVERER AND THEIR APPRECIATION OF THE GREAT ACHIEVEMENTS OF THE FOUR COMPLETED CENTURIES OF AMERICAN LIFE.

Colorado was the first state to make Columbus Day an official holiday, and fourteen other states followed suit within five years. In 1934, President Franklin Delano Roosevelt made Columbus Day a national holiday, and in 1971, Congress decided that it would be observed on the second Monday of October each year.

HEY, WHAT ABOUT LEIF?!

Norwegian immigrants were a little salty about all the recognition Columbus was getting. If any explorer was going to get a holiday, they thought it should be Leif Erikson. Though Erikson was born in Iceland, his grandfather was from Norway, so Norwegians claimed him, too. He'd crossed the ocean five hundred years earlier, and unlike Columbus, he'd landed in North America! (Erikson actually landed in what is now Newfoundland, Canada, so it still wasn't the United States, but at least it was closer.)

In 1925, President Calvin Coolidge gave a speech at the Minnesota State Fair and acknowledged that it was actually Erikson who first crossed the ocean from Europe to land in the Americas. Several years later, Leif Erikson Day became a holiday in Wisconsin and Minnesota, both states with many Norwegian immigrants, and in 1954, the United States began observing Leif Erikson Day each year on October 9. If that's news to you, you're not alone. Unlike Columbus Day, Leif Erikson Day is not a federal holiday where you'd probably get the day off from work or school, so a lot of people don't know it exists.

As Americans have become aware of the details of Columbus's voyages and their impact on Native people, some have argued that the explorer should no longer be honored with holidays and monuments. In the summer of 2020, the United States saw nationwide protests against racism after a white police officer killed a Black man named George Floyd. In some cities, demonstrators demanded the removal of monuments and statues they said honored white supremacists and colonizers whose actions ultimately led to the slave trade. That included Columbus.

Protesters in Baltimore pulled down a statue of Columbus and dumped it into the city's harbor. In Byrd Park, in Richmond, Virginia, demonstrators tore down the Columbus statue, spray-painted it, set it on fire, and threw it in a nearby lake. Boston's Columbus statue was beheaded around the same time.

A decapitated statue of Christopher Columbus in Boston, June 2020

Other cities decided to take down statues on their own. Newark, New Jersey, removed its Columbus statue from Washington Park and made plans to replace it with a statue of Harriet Tubman, who led hundreds of enslaved people to freedom. The city of Columbia, South Carolina, decided to remove its Columbus statue from a park and relocate it to a museum, where it might one day be seen with more complete information about the explorer's legacy.

As for the holiday, some Italian Americans and others still see it as an opportunity to honor their heritage and pay tribute to an explorer whose voyages changed the world. Others say Columbus is simply not a man who should be honored. In 1977, the United Nations International Conference on Discrimination Against Indigenous Populations in the Americas recommended that Columbus Day be replaced with Indigenous Peoples' Day. In 1990, South Dakota became the first state to change the name of the holiday (to Native American Day), and a number of other states and cities have also decided to ditch Columbus Day in favor of a day to honor the people who were already in the Americas when he arrived.

Colorado decided to stop honoring Columbus, too, but still wanted to lift up Italian Americans somehow.

So in 2020, lawmakers there voted to replace Columbus Day with a holiday honoring Mother Frances
Xavier Cabrini, an Italian immigrant who founded
schools, hospitals, and orphanages throughout the
Americas. Colorado's Cabrini Day became the first
paid state holiday honoring a woman in the United
States. (All the others honor men.)

Francesca Cabrini

In October 2021, President Joe Biden issued a
national proclamation to commemorate Indigenous
Peoples' Day, becoming the first American president

to do so. Biden issued a proclamation about Columbus Day as well, but also noted the devastating effect his voyages had on Native people.

Today, we also acknowledge the painful history of wrongs and atrocities that many European explorers inflicted on Tribal Nations and Indigenous communities. It is a measure of our greatness as a Nation that we do not seek to bury these shameful episodes of our past—that we face them honestly, we bring them to the light, and we do all we can to address them.

A TIMELINE OF COLUMBUS
AND THE TAINO PEOPLE

21,000–23,000 BCE—America's earliest known people migrate from Asia.

7000–5000 BCE—Canoe navigators from the Yucatán area begin settlement of the Caribbean islands.

6TH CENTURY BCE—Pythagoras suggests that the earth is round, not flat.

4TH CENTURY BCE—Aristotle provides evidence to support the idea that the earth is round.

3RD CENTURY BCE—Eratosthenes uses geometry to determine that the earth is round and to figure out its approximate circumference.

2ND CENTURY CE—Ptolemy writes the *Almagest*, a book about planet shapes and motions.

AROUND 1000 CE—Leif Erikson lands in North America.

AROUND 1000 CE—Taino culture and body politic forms in the Caribbean islands.

1271–1295—Marco Polo travels through Asia; his adventures are then chronicled in *The Travels of Marco Polo*.

1451—Christopher Columbus is born in Genoa.

1474—Paolo dal Pozzo Toscanelli suggests to the king of Portugal that he'd be able to reach Asia by sailing west. The king refuses to pay for such a trip.

1476—Columbus travels to Portugal.

1479—Columbus marries Felipa Perestrello e Moniz.

1480—Their son Diego is born.

1484—Columbus tries—and fails—to get the king of Portugal to fund his voyage.

1485—Columbus's wife, Felipa, dies. He travels to Spain, hoping the king and queen there will support his trip.

1488—Another son, Hernando (also known as Fernando), is born to Christopher Columbus and Beatriz Enríquez de Arana.

1488—Bartolomeu Dias becomes the first explorer to round the tip of Africa.

1492—The king and queen of Spain agree to fund Columbus, and he sets out on his first voyage.

1493—Columbus returns to Spain in March and begins his second voyage in September.

1493—Taino cacique Caonabo declares the first Indigenous war against an invading colony. Columbus's Fort Navidad, the first such installation in the Americas, is destroyed and all Spanish soldiers are killed.

1496—Columbus returns to Spain after his second voyage. Oppression and enslavement of Taino people begins in earnest.

1498—Columbus begins his third voyage.

1500—Columbus is arrested and sent back to Spain.

1501—Amerigo Vespucci explores the southern part of South America and begins to recognize that this is not Asia but a separate continent.

1502—Nicolás de Ovando sets out for the Caribbean in February and takes over the settlement of Hispaniola.

In May, Columbus sets out on his fourth voyage.

1503—Ovando massacres the chiefs and many other people of the last major Taino territory in Hispaniola, led by the well-remembered woman cacique Anacaona, who is executed.

1504—Columbus returns to Spain after his fourth voyage.

1506—Columbus dies.

1512—Spanish conquest of Cuba begins. Chief cacique Hatuey rebels in Hispaniola and retreats to Cuba to warn the Cuban caciques. Hatuey is captured and burned to death by conquistadors. "Your only god is gold," he tells the Spanish, and refuses Christian baptism.

1519–1522—Ferdinand Magellan's crew circumnavigates the globe.

1519–1534—Taino cacique Enriquillo rebels against the Spanish encomienda. In 1534, he signs the first treaty between a Native people and Spain, the Treaty of Enriquillo. In Cuba, cacique Guamá is also in active rebellion.

1542—Spanish New Laws grant Native people freedom from enslavement. A period of recovery and survival begins.

1776—America begins fighting the Revolutionary War to gain independence from Great Britain.

1791—The new US capital is named after Columbus.

1828—Washington Irving publishes a fictionalized biography of Columbus, which becomes the source of much misinformation about the explorer.

1891—Eleven Italian immigrants are lynched in New Orleans, prompting some to call for a national day to honor Columbus as a way to show Americans that people of Italian descent are heroic and worthy of respect.

1892—President Benjamin Harrison calls for a national observance of Columbus Day.

1892—On the four hundredth anniversary of Columbus's first voyage, writers and historians take a closer look at the documents from his voyages, prompting some to question his legacy.

1907—Colorado becomes the first state to recognize Columbus Day, and other states follow suit.

1925—President Calvin Coolidge gives a speech in Minnesota, acknowledging that Leif Erikson reached the Americas before Columbus did.

1934—President Franklin Delano Roosevelt makes Columbus Day a federal holiday.

1954—The United States begins celebrating Leif Erikson Day each year on October 9.

1971—Congress decides that Columbus Day will be observed each year on the second Monday of October.

1977—The United Nations International Conference on Discrimination Against Indigenous Populations in the Americas recommends that Columbus Day be replaced with Indigenous Peoples' Day.

1990—South Dakota replaces Columbus Day with Native American Day.

1992—Native people in the Americas vigorously protest the planned Columbus Quincentenary; the Taino Nation of the Antilles publicly declares its continuous existence.

2020—Nationwide protests after the police killing of George Floyd lead to the destruction and removal of some statues honoring Columbus.

2021—Joe Biden becomes the first US president to issue a national proclamation commemorating Indigenous Peoples' Day.

AUTHOR'S NOTE FROM KATE MESSNER

It's hard to find a historical figure with more myths swirling around him than Christopher Columbus. Like most Americans my age, when I was in elementary school, I was taught about the explorer who "discovered" the Americas. It would be decades before I'd read the historical documents that tell the true story of his voyages and the impact they had on the Taino and other Native people.

The stories I'd read—about how Columbus was the only one who knew the world was round, how he discovered lands no one had ever seen before— weren't just inaccurate. They also served to erase the true story of people who had lived in what are now the Americas for thousands of years. I'm grateful for the opportunity to write about the real history of Columbus and the Taino people, and I hope it's a story you'll share.

As soon as the History Smashers series launched, I started getting requests in my in-box from teachers, librarians, and families. When was I going to write about Columbus? But I knew this wasn't a book I could write alone. After reading about the work of Dr. José Barreiro, a writer, historian, and Taino elder, I reached out to ask if he might be interested in collaborating with me, and I'm beyond grateful that he said yes. Special thanks to Dr. Barreiro's grandson Karakwatiron Hatuey Barreiro (Mohawk) for his help as an early reader as well.

Dr. Barreiro's work here and elsewhere helps to smash what may be the most important myth of all surrounding this story and shares the truth: the Taino people are still here.

AUTHOR'S NOTE FROM JOSÉ BARREIRO

I love our Taino stories.

We need to know where we come from. For human beings, this is a core curiosity. I grew up among guajiro people, in a region of Cuba called Camagüey. Guajiro are the people of the land, the natural Cubans. My old people knew the healing herbs, how to plant the old crops like yuca (manioc), corn, and beans, and they could tell by the phases of the moon (the grandmother) when and where to harvest in the forest. They could hunt and they could fish. Some knew old massage methods (called sobar), and others could tell stories about little people, jigues, and about shape-shifters, cagüeiro.

They also told about a great hero of ours, specially honoring the cacique, or chief, Hatuey, who died defending our lands against the conquistadors. When I asked about these old ways, my grandfather would say, "Oh, that comes from the old Indians." I remembered the stories and always wondered about those "old Indians," our ancestors. In time, I read the histories of the Native people of our Caribbean islands and relived many more stories of our Taino ancestors. I wrote these stories into a novel, called *Taino*.

I love our Taino stories; they tell us much about who we are. I promised myself I would never forget our history.

RECOMMENDED READING

"1492: An Ongoing Voyage," from the Library of Congress
loc.gov/exhibits/1492

Higuayagua: Taíno of the Caribbean
unionhiwayawa.com

An Indigenous Peoples' History of the United States for Young People
by Roxanne Dunbar-Ortiz, adapted by Jean Mendoza and
Debbie Reese (Beacon Press, 2019)

The United Confederation of Taíno People
uctp.org

SELECTED BIBLIOGRAPHY

Alegría, Ricardo E. "Aspectos de la cultura de los indios taínos de las Antillas Mayores en la documentación etno-histórica." In *La cultura taína*, 117–136. Madrid: Sociedad Estatal Quinto Centenario y Turner Libros, 1989.

Alegría, Ricardo E. *Ball Courts and Ceremonial Plazas in the West Indies*. New Haven, CT: Yale University Press, 1983.

Anghiera, Peter Martyr d'. *De Orbe Novo: The Eight Decades of Peter Martyr D'Anghiera*. Translated by Francis Augustus MacNutt. New York: Burt Franklin, 1970.

Arrom, José Juan. *Mitología y artes prehispánicas de las Antillas*. Mexico: Siglo XXI, 1975.

Barreiro, José Juan. "Beyond the Myth of Extinction: The Hatuey Regiment." *KACIKE: The Journal of Caribbean Amerindian History and Anthropology*, 2004. archive.org/stream /KacikeJournal_34/barreiro_djvu.txt.

Barreiro, José Juan. "Taíno Survivals: Cacique Panchito, Caridad de los Indios, Cuba." In *Indigenous Resurgence in the Contemporary Caribbean: American Survival and Revival,* edited by Maximilian C. Forte, 21–39. New York: Peter Lang, 2006.

BBC News. "Colombian Anti-government Protesters Topple Columbus Statue." June 29, 2021. bbc.com/news/world-latin-america-57651833.

Brito, Christopher. "Harriet Tubman Monument Replacing a Christopher Columbus Statue in Newark Is 'Poetic,' Mayor Says." *CBS News,* June 21, 2021. cbsnews.com/news/newark-nj-harriet-tubman-statue-christopher-columbus.

Campbell, Colin, and Emily Opilo. "Christopher Columbus Statue near Little Italy Brought Down, Tossed into Baltimore's Inner Harbor." *Baltimore Sun,* July 4, 2020. baltimoresun.com/maryland/baltimore-city/bs-md-ci-columbus-statue-20200705-xc4bhthfhjaflifz72org2lrhy-story.html.

Cassá, Roberto. *Historia social y económica de la República Dominicana.* 2nd ed. 2 vols. Santo Domingo: Editora Alfa y Omega, 1992.

Cassá, Roberto. *Los Taínos de la Española.* Santo Domingo: Editora de la Universidad Autónoma de Santo Domingo, 1974.

Coleman, Rebecca. "The Timeline History of Celebrating (and Not Celebrating) Columbus Day." *Smithsonian Magazine,* October 10, 2016. smithsonianmag.com/history/timeline-history-celebrating-and-not-celebrating-columbus-day-180960736.

Colón, Fernando. *The Life of the Admiral Christopher Columbus, by his son Ferdinand*. Translated and annotated by Benjamin Keen. New Brunswick, NJ: Rutgers University Press, 1959. (Contains an English translation of Fray Ramón Pané's *Relación acerca de la antigüedades de los Indios*.)

Columbus, Christopher. *The Four Voyages of Christopher Columbus*. Edited and translated by J. M. Cohen. London: Penguin, 1969.

Ebrahimji, Alisha. "Colorado Will Replace Columbus Day with Cabrini Day, the First Paid State Holiday Recognizing a Woman in the US." *CNN*, March 11, 2020. cnn.com/2020/03/11/us /colorado-columbus-day-cabrini-day-trnd/index.html.

Fastenau, Stephen. "Columbia Plans to House Columbus Statue at State Museum, a Year After Removal from Park." *Columbia Post and Courier*, June 23, 2021. postandcourier.com/columbia /news/columbia-plans-to-house-columbus-statue-at-state -museum-a-year-after-removal-from-park/article_02b45d46 -d42f-11eb-b020-3b4b7c4b8f06.html.

Gandhi, Lakshmi. "How Columbus Sailed Into U.S. History, Thanks to Italians." NPR *CodeSwitch*, October 14, 2013. npr.org /sections/codeswitch/2013/10/14/232120128/how-columbus -sailed-into-u-s-history-thanks-to-italians.

Handwerk, Brian. "Why Christopher Columbus Was the Perfect Icon for a New Nation Looking for a Hero." *Smithsonian Magazine*, October 9, 2015. smithsonianmag.com/history/why -christopher-columbus-was-perfect-icon-new-nation-looking -hero-180956887.

Hanke, Lewis. *The First Social Experiments in America*. Cambridge, MA: Harvard University Press, 1935.

Indian Country Today. "Why Is Columbus Day a Thing? The History Behind the 'Holiday.'" September 13, 2018. indiancountrytoday .com/archive/why-is-columbus-day-a-thing-the-history -behind-the-holiday.

Las Casas, Fray Bartolomé de. *Historia de las Indias.* Vols. 1–3 of *Obras Completas,* compiled by Paulino Castañeda, Carlos de Rueda, and Carmen Godínez e Inmaculada de la Corte. Madrid: Alianza Editorial, 1995.

Las Casas, Fray Bartolomé de. *Apologética Historia Sumaria.* Vols. 6–8 of *Obras Completas,* compiled by Paulino Castañeda, Carlos de Rueda, and Carmen Godínez e Inmaculada de la Corte. Madrid: Alianza Editorial, 1995.

Library of Congress. "Columbus Day." Today in History. Accessed July 14, 2021. loc.gov/item/today-in-history/october-12.

Machemer, Theresa. "Christopher Columbus Statues Beheaded, Pulled Down Across America." *Smithsonian Magazine,* June 12, 2020. smithsonianmag.com/smart-news/christopher -columbus-statues-beheaded-torn-down-180975079.

Mann, Charles C. *1491: New Revelations of the Americas Before Columbus.* New York: Vintage Books, 2005.

Mann, Charles C. *1493: Uncovering the New World Columbus Created.* New York: Alfred A. Knopf, 2011.

Morgan, Edmund S. "Columbus' Confusion About the New World." *Smithsonian Magazine,* October 2009. smithsonianmag.com /travel/columbus-confusion-about-the-new-world-140132422.

NBC12. "Christopher Columbus Statue Torn Down, Thrown in Lake by Protesters." June 10, 2020. nbc12.com/2020/06/09 /christopher-columbus-statue-torn-down-thrown-lake-by -protesters.

Oviedo y Valdés, Gonzalo Fernández de. *Historia general y natural de las Indias.* 5 vols. Biblioteca de Autores Españoles, vols. 117–121. Madrid: Gráficas Orbe, 1959. First published 1535.

Palmer, Alex. "This Culture, Once Believed Extinct, Is Flourishing." *Smithsonian Magazine,* August 23, 2018. smithsonianmag .com/smithsonian-institution/culture-once-believed-extinct -flourishing-180970101.

Philips, William D., Jr., and Carla Rahn Phillips. *The Worlds of Christopher Columbus.* Cambridge: Cambridge University Press, 1992.

Quill, Elizabeth. "Did This Map Guide Columbus?" *Smithsonian Magazine,* June 2015. smithsonianmag.com/history/did-this -map-guide-columbus-180955295.

Robiou Lamarche, Sebastián. *Encuentro con la mitologia taína.* San Juan: Editorial Punto y Coma, 1992.

Rouse, Irving. *The Tainos: Rise and Decline of the People Who Greeted Columbus.* New Haven, CT: Yale University Press, 1992.

Sauer, Carl Ortwin. *The Early Spanish Main.* Berkeley: University of
  California Press, 1992. First published 1966.

Sued-Badillo, Jalil. *La mujer indígena y su sociedad.* San Juan:
  Editorial Cultural, 1989.

Sutton, Jane. "Bones Tell Tale of Slain Serpent: Archeologist Links
  Columbus, Crocodile." *Los Angeles Times*, October 25, 1987.
  latimes.com/archives/la-xpm-1987-10-25-mn-16241-story
  .html.

Ulloa Hung, Jorge, and Roberto Valcárcel Rojas, eds. "Cuba. Indios
  después de Colón." *Indígenas e indios en el Caribe: Presencia,
  legado y studio.* Santo Domingo: Instituto Tecnológico de Santo
  Domingo, 2016.

Wei-Haas, Maya. "Stunning Footprints Push Back Human Arrival
  in Americas by Thousands of Years." *National Geographic,*
  September 21, 2021. nationalgeographic.com/history/article
  /fossil-footprints-challenge-theory-when-people-first-arrived
  -americas.

Wilson, Samuel M. *Hispaniola: Caribbean Chiefdoms in the Age of
  Columbus.* Tuscaloosa: University of Alabama Press, 1990.

Winkle, Timothy. "The Monument That Created Columbus."
  National Museum of American History. October 12, 2020.
  americanhistory.si.edu/blog/created-columbus.

Wright, Irene. *The Early History of Cuba, 1492–1586.* New York:
  Macmillan, 1916.

Zotigh, Dennis W., and Renee Gokey. "Rethinking How We Celebrate American History—Indigenous Peoples' Day." *Smithsonian Magazine*, October 12, 2020. smithsonianmag.com/blogs /national-museum-american-indian/2020/10/12/indigenous -peoples-day-updated2020.

IMAGE CREDITS

Andrews, E. Benjamin/Wikimedia Commons (p. 154); Artnet/ Wikimedia Commons (p. 15); José Barreiro (p. 147); Tim Bradbury/Getty Images (p. 159); John Carter Brown Library/ Wikimedia Commons (p. 132 right); Tomás Castelazo/ Wikimedia Commons (p. 75); Jos1950/Wikimedia Commons (p. 143); Mariner's Museum Collection/Wikimedia Commons (p. 138); Mariordo (Mario Roberto Durán Ortiz)/Wikimedia Commons (p. 128); Luke McKernan/Wikimedia Commons (p. 38); Metropolitan Museum of Art/Wikimedia Commons (p. 14); Miguel Angel/Wikimedia Commons (p. 127); National Museum of Art, Architecture and Design, Norway/Wikimedia Commons (p. 5); National Park Service (p. 22); National Portrait Gallery/Wikimedia Commons (p. 87); NMAI Mark Raymond Harrington/National Museum of the American Indian, Smithsonian Institution (N01404) (p. 145); NMAI Photo Services/Smithsonian National Museum of the American Indian (12/7442) (p. 71); Wikimedia Commons (pp. 113, 132 left, 161)

INDEX

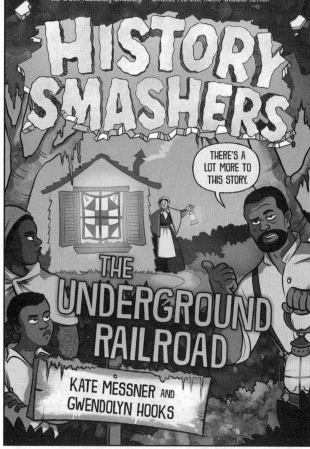

You've probably heard stories about the Underground Railroad, the secret network of helpers who provided aid to people escaping from slavery. Tales from this chapter of American history are often full of excitement, with freedom seekers racing through the darkness, lanterns hung in windows, and hidden rooms with sneaky getaway tunnels. Maybe you've read about Harriet Tubman, who escaped from slavery and then led hundreds of others to do the same. Or Quaker families who risked everything to help, breaking laws they knew were unjust.

But only some of those stories are true. People really did escape from slavery. In the first half of the nineteenth century, thousands found their way to freedom every year. And some of them did get help, but not from a super-organized national group that provided detailed maps of safe houses. Instead, they found shelter with people who were part of loosely connected antislavery networks, or they got unexpected aid from people who weren't associated with those groups at all. Some of the most heroic helpers were left out of history books entirely, while others claimed more credit than they deserved. And most people who escaped from slavery had to do it on their own, with courage, cleverness, and determination.

The true story of the Underground Railroad involves a lot more than nighttime escapes and secret rooms. It's a story of resistance and resilience—one that begins even before the first enslaved people were brought to the Americas.

ONE
HOW SLAVERY CAME TO AMERICA

A true history of slavery and resistance begins with the story of the people who were enslaved. Before Africans were taken to the Americas, they lived rich and varied lives as citizens of many different nations. They crafted tools and weapons out of iron and made clothing from the woven fibers of palm leaves. Those who lived near the ocean fished and made salt by boiling seawater in clay jars.

Other African people were farmers. They grew rice, yams, and a kind of grain called millet. They raised oxen, cows, horses, pigs, goats, and dogs. They brought their crops and animals to huge markets, where thousands of people came to find the goods their families needed.

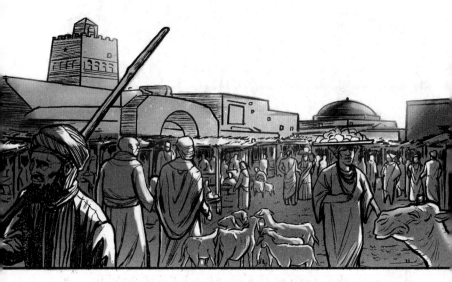

Africa had vibrant economies and organized governments. Even in big kingdoms, many people were involved in decision-making. The kingdoms of Africa had figured out a thing or two about democracy before the United States of America was even a thought, much less a nation on a map.

All that time, African people were making art and developing scientific ideas. They built several great, huge libraries and passed down knowledge from generation to generation. Researchers have rediscovered thousands of ancient African manuscripts, focused on everything from religion to mathematics to astronomy.

Slavery was also part of life in Africa, and that comes as a surprise to some people. But America didn't invent slavery. The practice goes all the way back to ancient Greece and Rome, and Africa, too. Historically, people hadn't been enslaved based on the color of their skin. In ancient times, slavery was most often a way to take advantage of those who had been captured during war.

An ancient Roman mosaic shows
two enslaved men pouring wine.

That began to change in the 1400s, when Portugal started bringing enslaved people from Africa to Europe. You might be wondering how anyone could justify stealing people away from their homes and forcing them to work on another continent, even way back then. Europeans tried to justify it by claiming that African people were inferior to people from Europe.

A Portuguese writer likely helped that idea along. Gomes Eanes de Zurara was a royal chronicler, which meant he was in charge of writing the official history of his nation. He wrote that African people were living "like beasts, without any custom of reasonable beings." He said that if people weren't living peacefully under a government with laws, they really weren't people at all, so it was fine to enslave them.

We know none of that was true. African people had kingdoms and thriving economies, along with great knowledge of science, math, and architecture. Many people in Europe certainly knew that, too. But the racist idea that Africans were somehow inferior took hold. Other Europeans wrote similar things. For centuries, the works of Europeans erased the real history of African people and replaced it with one that would justify their enslavement.

At first, this new slave trade mostly brought African people to Portugal and Spain. Then Christopher Columbus came along.

There are enough myths about Columbus to fill an entire book, but for now, it's enough to know that his explorations opened the door on a whole new era of enslavement. At first, Columbus was sending enslaved people from the Caribbean back to Europe. These were Taino men and women he'd captured from the islands where they'd lived their whole lives.

The Spanish enslaved Native people and forced them to work in the Caribbean, too, in gold mines on the island of Hispaniola.

When those early European explorers arrived in the Americas, they brought along diseases. Native people had no immunity to the new germs, so smallpox and other illnesses ravaged Hispaniola. Less than twenty years after the arrival of Columbus, the Native population had dropped from as many as three million to just about twenty-five thousand who were still able to work.

That's when the Spanish began bringing enslaved people across the ocean, a practice that was marked by cruelty and brutality at every stage. In 1510, King Ferdinand II gave his approval for fifty enslaved African people to be sent from Spain to Hispaniola to work in the gold mines.

... THE BEST AND STRONGEST AVAILABLE!

Three weeks later, the king ordered another two hundred enslaved people to be shipped across the sea under cramped, filthy conditions and forced to work in the mines. This was the beginning of the Atlantic slave trade. Soon slave traders would begin capturing people in Africa and taking them straight to the Caribbean. Over the next 350 years, 12.5 million African people were sold into slavery in the Americas.

THE STORY OF HANDSOME JOHN

You might assume that every Black person who traveled to the Americas was enslaved, but that wasn't the case. Some came as free men, like Juan Garrido, who set sail for the Caribbean on a Spanish ship in the early 1500s, when he was just fifteen years old. Garrido's nickname was Handsome John. (We don't have any pictures of him from that time period, so you'll have to imagine him to decide if the name fit.)

It's not clear how Garrido ended up joining the Spanish. Some historians think he may have been the son of an African king who gave him the job of doing business with the Europeans. It's also possible that he was enslaved and joined the Spanish soldiers in exchange for freedom.

Garrido spent six years in Hispaniola before he went with explorer Juan Ponce de León on a mission to search for gold. They traveled to Puerto Rico and later landed on the peninsula we now call Florida. They claimed it for Spain, but the Calusa people, whose ancestors had lived there for thousands of years, forced them to leave.

Garrido also sailed with Hernán Cortés, a Spanish conquistador, or conqueror, who invaded Mexico and attacked the Aztec people in 1519. Later, Garrido returned to Florida with Ponce de León and a couple hundred settlers, hoping to set up a colony. Native people fought them off again, this time fatally wounding Ponce de León. Garrido escaped and continued to serve with the Spanish.

The slave trade grew so quickly that part of West Africa became known as the Slave Coast: a two-hundred-mile-long stretch that included the modern-day nations of Togo, Benin, and Nigeria. African rulers and merchants made deals with slave traders, sometimes selling their own people into slavery across the sea. The trade increased with the growth of the sugar industry in Brazil and the Caribbean. Sugar plantations required a lot of labor.

As the slave trade grew, the Dutch and the English were also colonizing North America, invading lands that had been home to Native people for generations. They wanted free labor, and merchants eager to make money jumped at the chance to provide it. By 1740, Great Britain was sending more than thirty slave ships to Africa each year, enslaving tens of thousands of people and forcing them on a nightmare journey across the sea.

THE POWER OF WORDS

One of the ways white Europeans and Americans tried to justify slavery was by dehumanizing the people they enslaved, talking about them as if they weren't people at all. Fugitive slave advertisements and other documents written by enslavers refer to the people they enslaved as everything from "beasts" to "creatures" to "slaves." Almost never as people.

But they were people. So in this book, unless we're using the word "slave" as historical language in a quote from a primary source, that's how we'll talk about them, as people. They were not slaves. They were people who were enslaved.

We'll also avoid using the words "runaway" and "fugitive" to describe those who escaped from slavery. Those words make people sound like criminals simply because they rejected the idea that it was fine for one person to own another. "Freedom seekers" feels like a more appropriate choice of words, so that's what you'll find in this book unless it's a quote or another reference from that time period.

FUGITIVES

RUNAWAYS

FREEDOM SEEKERS

SMASH MORE STORIES!

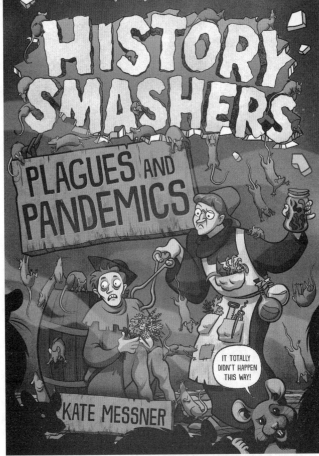

TURN THE PAGE FOR A PEEK AT ANOTHER GREAT BOOK IN THE HISTORY SMASHERS SERIES!

You've probably heard about the Black Death and other big disease outbreaks in history. If you're reading this book, you've probably even lived through one yourself.

Widespread outbreaks of illnesses make history because they can alter populations, power structures, and government policies. They've taught us about science and changed the way we deal with everything from throwing away garbage to preventing disease and caring for the sick.

But some of the stories told about outbreaks are just plain wrong. A long time ago, people were certain that diseases were caused by angry gods or bad-smelling air. If you were sick, friends might advise you to drink wine or eat crushed emeralds. If those cures didn't work, you might have tried putting pig bladders full of hot water under your armpits!

Thankfully, most of those way-off-base remedies are a thing of the past. Today, we know that many diseases are caused by tiny organisms known as microbes, such as bacteria and viruses. And today, most people—but not all—listen to science instead of myths when it comes to understanding illnesses and treatments. Still, the history of plagues and pandemics is full of stories that need smashing, starting with ancient times and continuing through today. So let's get to work. . . .

ONE
ANCIENT AILMENTS

Microbes have been around a lot longer than people, and they'll probably be around well after we're gone. Most microbes are harmless or beneficial. They help us digest food and fight off infection. But microbes can also make us sick.

When lots of people get sick from the same microbe at the same time, that's called an epidemic.

When an epidemic spreads around the world,
it's called a pandemic.

The first recorded epidemics in history go all the way back to ancient times. *The Epic of Gilgamesh,* a poem written in ancient Mesopotamia, mentioned a visit from the god of pestilence (disease) around 2000 BCE. Ancient Egyptian and Chinese writings also refer to pestilence.

One of the first well-documented epidemics was the Plague of Athens, which happened in 430 BCE. The Greek city-state of Athens was fighting Sparta in the Peloponnesian War, and Athens had built walls around the city. People from the countryside moved inside to be protected, creating a super-crowded place where disease could spread easily.

A general and historian named Thucydides wrote that a quarter of the Athenian army died. What made them sick? We don't know, because people didn't understand diseases well at that time, but we can make some guesses based on ancient writings.

Fortunately, Thucydides himself got sick! While this was rotten news for him, it was good news for modern scientists and historians who have tried to piece together what happened in Athens. These are the symptoms Thucydides wrote down:

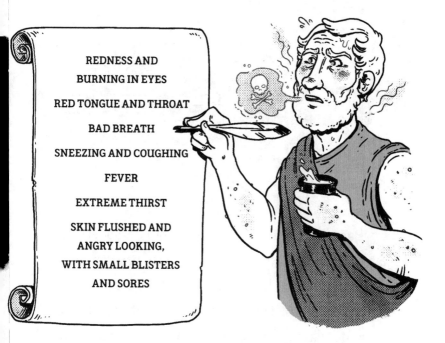

REDNESS AND
BURNING IN EYES

RED TONGUE AND THROAT

BAD BREATH

SNEEZING AND COUGHING

FEVER

EXTREME THIRST

SKIN FLUSHED AND
ANGRY LOOKING,
WITH SMALL BLISTERS
AND SORES

Based on the list of symptoms, modern-day experts think the disease might have been smallpox or measles. Even though it's called the Plague of Athens, they don't think it's likely that people had bubonic plague, because that disease produces big bulges on the body, called buboes, which would have been hard for old Thucydides to ignore in his descriptions. Whatever it was, the epidemic devastated Athens, which lost the war. It was the beginning of the end for what had been the most powerful city-state in Greece . . . all because of a microbe, a tiny germ that no one could even see.

THE MUMMIES HAD MALARIA

Some of ancient Egypt's disease history is recorded in the bodies of preserved mummies. Around 6000 BCE, when people started farming in Egypt, they noticed that the Nile River flooded once a year, swamping the valley on both sides. The flooding was great for creating fertile soil for crops, but it was also perfect for mosquitoes, which breed in standing, shallow water. Mosquitoes can carry a tiny parasite that causes a disease we now call malaria.

✸ In 1922, archaeologist Howard Carter opened the inner shrine of the tomb of King Tutankhamen, better known as King Tut. Scientists now believe the king had malaria before he died at age nineteen.

Papyrus scrolls written by doctors in ancient Egypt talk about "the pest of the year," an illness that showed up when the river flooded. Was it malaria? Thousands of years later, some well-preserved mummies still held the answer to that question. Archaeologists studied a group of mummies from one area of Egypt and found that almost half of them showed evidence of being infected with malaria.

The more people travel, the more diseases can spread. As ancient trade routes opened up, microbes hitched a ride on ships and caravans carrying silk and spices. And when armies traveled during wartime, their crowded camps were a perfect breeding ground for bacteria and viruses.

Back then people didn't know what was making them sick. The ancient Greeks blamed angry gods and believed that if you were ill, you needed to patch things up with the gods so they'd make you well again. So they built asclepeions, which were sort of half shrines and half hospitals where sick people could go to ask priests for help with cures. Asclepeions were located in pretty country settings with clean air and pure water, and people who went there were encouraged to eat a healthy diet, exercise, and get lots of rest. Those practices were probably why some of the sick got better—not because the priests there had some sort of direct line to the gods.

If you think being treated at an asclepeion sounds pretty great, there's one more thing you should know: one of the cures involved having snakes slither over you. The snakes were considered sacred and could supposedly make people well . . . somehow.

HOW MANY STORIES HAVE YOU **SMASHED**?

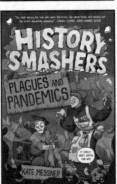